Santa Dolls & Figurines Price Guide

Antique to Contemporary

by Polly and Pam Judd

This is a sculpted reproduction of one of the paintings of Thomas Nast published by Harper's Weekly *in the 1860s. It was made by the Duncan Royale Company. (See page 131).*

Published by **Hobby House Press** Grantsville Maryland 21536

Dedication

This book is dedicated to the Endless Hills Doll and Toy Collectors Club of Northeastern Pennsylvania. It is also dedicated to the participants of the Region 13 Conference of the United Federation of Doll Collectors Inc. This Conference, which had as its theme, "500 Years Young," was held October 23 to 24, 1992.

In the beginning, this book was a "gleam" in the eyes of Mary Ann Hall. Phyllis Bechtold, Director of Region 13, jumped right in and untiringly worked to expedite Mary Ann's idea. Both of them were there when the authors needed them, as were many other members of the Endless Hills Doll and Toy Collectors Club. The excitement grew as Jane Anderson, Jayne Keller and others sent in pictures of their Santa Claus collections. The authors want to thank the entire doll club for its diligent efforts.

David K. Bausch permitted us to photograph his unusual and wonderful Santa Claus collection.

Margaret Benike provided pictures and information to us.

Shirley Karaba not only let us photograph her dolls, but she chauffeured us around when we needed to be.

Wally, Donna, Eryn and Kyle Judd helped with pictures, inspiration and love.

We were delighted and very excited to have John Axe as the editor of this book. He is a very dear friend and a wonderful editor and writer.

The following people sent photographs, allowed us to photograph, provided information or helped us in other ways: Charles Backus, Yoshiko Baker, Joyce Barth, Don Beck, John Bechtold, Marlene Brenner, Laura May Brown, Barbara and Jim Comienski, Beverly Cope, Carole Correll, Joan L. Dautch, De Fina Auctions, Max E. Duncan, Marianne Gardner, C.M. Geppi, C. Gordon Hitchings, Jean D. Hagerty, Nancy Harmon, Lu Lane, McMasters Productions, Robert M. Merch, Helene Marlowe, Pat Parton, J.L. Roush, Peggy Tombro, June and Dennis Tressler, Rosalie Whyel, Patricia L. Wilson, Linda Yonker, and Chuck Young.

We thank them all.

Additional copies of this book may be purchased at $14.95 from
Hobby House Press
One Corporate Drive
Grantsville, Maryland 21536
or from your favorite bookstore or dealer.
Please add $4.75 per copy for postage.

Printed in the United States of America
ISBN: 0-87588-420-2

Table of Contents

Foreword 4

System Used for Pricing Dolls and Figures 5

19th and Turn-of-the-20th Century Santas 6

Santa Claus from 1911-1930 19

Santa Claus from 1931-1950 39

Santa Claus from 1951-1970 57

Santa Claus from 1971 to the Present 79

Santa on Paper 101

Contemporary Doll Artist's Santa Clauses 116

Santa Claus and Other Bearers of Gifts
  from Around the World 125

Revised Price Guide 151

Index 159

COVER DESCRIPTION: Schoenhut Display Santa Claus. See *Illustration 32. Rosalie Whyel Museum of Doll Art, Bellevue, Washington. Photograph by Charles Backus.*

Foreword

Santa Claus has played a major role in many Christmas celebrations since the 19th century. Although the name *Santa Claus* originated in the United States, the "spirit" he represents is called by many other names in other countries around the world. This book documents these names and some of the changes in Santa Claus and other Christmas-time gift givers.

Since the celebration of Christmas comes during the Winter Solstice when there are more hours of darkness in the northern hemisphere, there is time for holidays, feasting after the harvest, celebrations, and gift giving. Along with these gifts, homes and other buildings are decorated with ornaments, bright lights and images of Santa Claus. Although many families pass these ornaments, lights and figures from one generation to another, some of them have entered the antique and collectible markets.

The "Art of Christmas Past" has become very desirable as collectibles. When collectors seek images of Santa Claus, they want information about his history and the various costumes that he wore. This book serves as an Identification, Price and Information Guide. It also explains Gift-Givers from other countries and the legends which surround them.

The authors have collected Santa Clauses for many years. They have studied the legends, and have enjoyed seeking out the "Jolly Man in the Red Suit" in many countries. Most of all they enjoy knowing that Santa Claus not only brings gifts, but he also brings smiles and happiness to the young and old around the world.

About the Authors

Both mother and daughter enjoy collecting dolls and learning more about dolls as a team. It was understandable that their research efforts and their love of sharing doll information would progress from writing articles for the leading doll collector's magazines to a book. Their first book, *Hard Plastic Dolls, Volume I*, and the hundreds of letters of encouragement that they received started them on a dozen year odyssey of writing a total of seven books. Both skilled researchers, Polly says "It just came 'naturally' that my daughter, Pam, and I write about the hobby we enjoy so much—doll collecting."

System Used for Pricing Dolls and Figures

Making, buying and collecting holiday decorations have been part of a traditional family life in the United States for most of the 19th and 20th centuries. With the advent of the "Country" look in home decoration, there has been a new interest in Santa Claus memorabilia in recent years. Prices have risen accordingly.

There has also been an increase in production of Santa Claus dolls and figures by modern artists working in many mediums. These are selling well. They will be the antiques and collectibles of tomorrow. They are priced in this book at, or near, their original selling prices, since they are so recent.

For each illustration there is a range of prices depending on the condition of the doll or figure. Mint dolls will command higher prices and dolls in poor condition will be about one-third to one-half the lowest price.

As happens in other areas of the art world, the work of well-known companies or artists will command higher prices. Recent auction prices have soared on coveted Santa Claus items. In general, in the past few years prices have climbed as more collectors have become interested in this memorabilia. The "American Santa Claus" is now known around the world, and collectors in other countries are now competing for the antique and collectible Santas.

In general, the early German figures command the highest prices. American mechanical toy Santas have escalated in price in recent years. The prices of the Santas made in Japan during the 1920s and the 1930s are lower in general than the German and American ones, but there has been intense interest in them recently, and they have risen considerably in the last two or three years.

The prices and photographs of the Santas in this book have been gathered from dealers and collectors from all over the United States. Auction prices have been monitored. Local prices vary with the highest prices reported on the East Coast, West Coast, Florida and southwest states.

Although an Althof-Bergman "Santa in Sleigh" went for $104,000 in April, 1991, this is an exception.

The authors realize that all the different Santas that have been made cannot be shown in this book; however, it is hoped that collectors will understand the different types available and can adjust the prices to their own collection or future purchases.

We hope you enjoy encountering the wide range of Santas in this book as much as we have enjoyed presenting them.

Chapter 1   *In the Beginning...*

19th and Turn-of-the-20th Century Santas

The Santa Claus the world knows today derives from many Christian religious, environmental and cultural gift-bearing traditions around the world. However, in many ways Santa Claus as "the jolly man in the red suit with a sleigh pulled by reindeer from the North Pole" comes from the fertile imaginations of American writers, authors and artists. They created this kind man to fill the wishes of children everywhere.

Washington Irving in 1809 was the first to write about the present concept of Santa Claus in *A History of New York from the Beginning of the World to the End of the Dutch Dynasty*. Irving's view was based on the legends of the Dutch St. Nicholas. In 1823 Dr. Clement Clarke Moore wrote the famous poem "A Visit from St. Nicholas."

In the 1860s Thomas Nast began a series of 30 or more portraits of Santa Claus in *Harper's Weekly Magazine*. These drawings appeared over a period of 22 years, and Santa Claus took on the modern characteristics that the world knows now. Nast used himself as a model, and his conception of Santa Claus came from traditions of his Bavarian youth.

Another American artist, Norman Rockwell, was the first to picture Santa as an international figure. He drew him many times, and one of his finest paintings shows Santa Claus plotting his travels on a globe. (See *Illustration 56*.) As inventive methods of communication and travel appeared, the idea that the American version of Santa Claus visited the entire world bearing gifts spread from country to country.

The photographs in this chapter show the early images of Santa Claus from the 19th century and early 20th century. These are the stooped and often grotesque, but still lovable, old man image of Santa on his journeys. Many of these figures were made in Germany. Some of them carry switches or travel with a companion carrying switches. Germans were wonderfully inventive toymakers and many of their dolls and figures are now considered "works of art."

These Santa Clauses are highly valued today. They are hard to find and expensive to buy. Lucky are the descendants of the families who have passed down their childhood images of Santa Claus from generation to generation.

White Wadding Santa: 7in (18cm); cardboard body; Father Christmas die-cut scrap face; carries both a bundle of sticks and bag for gifts; turn-of-the-century. SEE: *Illustration 1. McMasters Productions.*

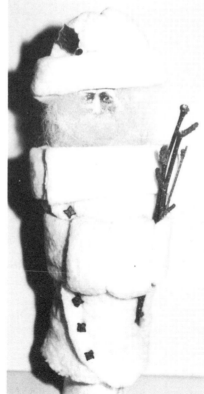

White Father Christmas: 10in (25cm); die-cut scrap face; wadded cotton costume; mohair wig; red buttons on coat; rolled cardboard body; carrying switches; late 1800s.

This type of doll has often been reproduced over the years.
SEE: *Illustration 2. David Bausch Collection.*

7

Godey's Lady's Book Father Christmas: 13in (33cm); pine cone body; papier-mâché molded and painted face; fur hair and beard; burlap bag full of toys including a doll, jester, Jack-in-the-box; clothespin soldier.

This Father Christmas was made by Polly Judd from the instructions given in the *Godey's Lady's Book*, December 1868, page 536.

Several doll artists have made and sold copies of this Santa Claus.

Vogue Miss Ginny Christmas Dolls: 14in (36cm) vinyl body and head; dressed in fur-trimmed velvet costumes; all-original; late 1960s.

MARKS: None on dolls.

SEE: *Illustration 3.*

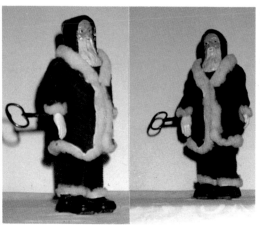

Ives Walking Doll: 10in (25cm); zinc head; wood body; iron feet; wooden rollers; brown Santa costume with fur trim; key wind mechanism; 1875.
SEE: *Illustration 4. David Bausch Collection.*

FRONT   BACK

E.S. Peck Santa Claus: Printed cloth for cutting and sewing; the design patented in December 1889.

By the end of the 19th century, the technique of printing on cloth in multi-colors had been perfected. Printers created wonderful cut-out cloth dolls which could be purchased by the yard. For this Santa, the artist included "the new patriotic look" and Santa carried the American flag along with a Chinese doll, a German peg doll and a drum; blue pants; brown fur hat.

MARKS: "Make your own Doll. Let every child in the Country have one" printed between the front and back of doll.

SEE: *Illustration 5. Nancy E. Harmon Collection.*

Wadding Santa Claus: 13in (33cm); unusual papier-mâché face; dark painted eyebrows; claw-like hands covered with paper; original moss basket; handle wrapped with holly; packages in basket; 1895.

The German Santa makers often painted red lines on the forehead to make the figure seem more "severe."

This Santa was listed in an 1895 Butler Bros. catalog.

SEE: *Illustration 6. Jane Anderson Collection.*

Santa on Skis: 3in (8cm); die-cut scrap face; cotton wadding hood and coat; corrugated paper legs; lavender short pants; wooden skis.

It is difficult to give the age of this doll. The die-cut seems to be from the early 19th century; however, these die-cuts and cotton wadding Santas were widely copied in the 20th century.

MARKS: None.

SEE: *Illustration 7. Margaret Benike Collection.*

Mechanical Bank: 6in (15cm) high; cast iron; American-made by J. and E. Stevens; Santa's costume is the long robe of the period; 1889.

A coin is placed in Santa's hand. A button in the back propels the coin into the bank.

Later versions of this bank have "Santa Claus" embossed on the base.

SEE: *Illustration 8. Don Beck Collection.*

Belsnickle

A Belsnickle is a "Pennsylvania Dutch" (German) name for the German Weichnachtsmann, sometimes called Christmann (see *Illustration 234.*) There are many different legends about Belsnickle, but most of them agree that he went from door to door with a pocket full of goodies. Some of the legends say he also carried a pocketful of sticks, while other legends say that he was accompanied by dark figures carrying the sticks.

There are variations on the spelling of Belsnickle. Some people spell it Belsnickel, and others call and spell the figure Pelze-Nicol.

Red Belsnickle (doll on right): 12½in (32cm); painted papier-mâché; black base sprayed with mica; goosefeather tree; turn-of-the-century. **Red Belsnickle** (doll on left): 8in (20cm); painted papier-mâché; black base sprayed with mica; goosefeather tree missing; 1920s.

In the 1930s and even later, reproductions of this Santa were made of molded cardboard. The cardboard is fastened together at the sides. They are not as valuable as the early ones.

MARKS: "Germany" printed on base.
SEE: *Illustration 9. J.L. Roush Collection.*

Belsnickle (figure on left): 11½in (29cm); hollow papier-mâché; white robe with mica sprinkled on it; green band at hem; green chenille trim around hat; Germany; circa 1900-1917.
Belsnickle (figure on right): 8½in (22cm); hollow papier-mâché; white robe with gold chenille trim around hat; carrying a goose feather tree; Germany; circa 1900-1917.
SEE: *Illustration 10. Jane Anderson Collection.*

Belsnickle: 8in (20cm); papier-mâché; bright red coat with sparkling white mica trim; face has excellent details for a doll this size; blue pants; German; 1890s. **SEE:** *Illustration 11. Peggy A. Tombro Collection.*

Silver Belsnickle: 7in (18cm); hollow, molded plaster-coated papier-mâché; feather branches inserted into a hole under his arm; painted white and sprinkled with mica; made from the 1870s to about the 1920s.
MARKS: None.
SEE: *Illustration 12.*

Belsnickle: 9in (23cm); molded papier-mâché; red stocking-type hat, white costume with gold trim; carrying goose feather tree; Germany; turn of the century.
MARKS: "35" in pencil.
SEE: *Illustration 13* (doll on left). *David Bausch Collection.*
Belsnickle: 9in (23cm); papier-mâché; costume painted gold and sprinkled with gold mica; straw Christmas tree; turn-of-the-century.
MARKS: "Germany" base.
SEE: *Illustration 13* (doll on right). *Phyllis S. Bechtold Collection.*

Belsnickle Candy Container: 18in (46cm); papier-mâché; gold coat sprinkled with mica; painted red band at bottom of coat; unusual molded beard; carries the traditional branch; German; circa 1892.
   This is an unusually large Belsnickle.
SEE: *Illustration 14. Jane P. Anderson Collection.*

The registered trademarks, the trademarks and copyrights appearing in italics//bold within this chapter belong to Art Fabric Mills.

Art Fabric Mills Christmas Tree Decorations: 6in (15cm); printed in oil colors on fine cloth; comes in one-piece with only one side to sew; to be filled with cotton or sawdust; dolls include:
1. *Santa Claus.*
2. *Dina, The Dark Secret*, also a cook.
3. *Bridget, The Fault-Finder*, also a Necessary Evil.
4. *Uncle*, I Can't Tell You about him because—.
5. *New Mail Baby*, You will like her because you cannot help it.
6. *The Newly Wed Kid* (not pictured).
Art Fabric Mills made many cloth dolls that could be bought by the piece for home sewing during the early part of the century.
SEE: *Illustration 15.* Advertisement 1907.

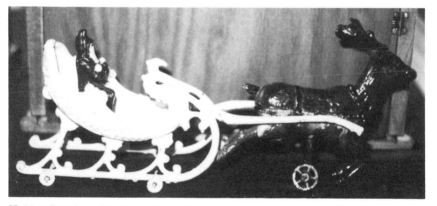

Hubley Cast Iron Sleigh and Santa Claus Pull Toy: 15in (38cm); white sleigh; painted Santa in red and white; one dark brown reindeer with one wheel; Santa's arms are movable; turn-of-the-century.

There is a reproduction set made about 1920. The quality is not as good.
MARKS: None.
SEE: *Illustration 16. Joan and Dan Dautch Memory Lane Antiques.*

French Walking Santa: 7in (18cm); papier-mâché face and hands; oval cardboard body; cast iron feet; key-wind mechanism; early part of the 20th century.
SEE: *Illustration 17. David Bausch Collection.*

Saint Nicholas: 25in (64cm); papier-mâché head; tightly stuffed body and legs; leather arms; fur hair and beard; painted eyes; green cotton twill tunic belted with gold buckle; red "frog" closures; red pants; leather-type high boots; fur-trimmed hat with red feather.
SEE: *Illustrations 18 and 19. Lu Lane Collection.*

St. Nicholas by Gebrüder Heubach: 13in (33cm); bisque face on original soft stuffed head and body; original crepe paper and flannel costume; bisque face has features of older man, painted blue eyes; incised wrinkles; closed mouth; applied beard; carrying canvas sack of antique toys and hickory sticks; early 1900s.

This is from the Heubach series of Christmas novelties and candy containers.
SEE: *Illustration 20. Mary Ann Hall Collection.*

All Bisque Santa: 4in (10cm); straight body; jointed arms and legs; paperweight eyes; pale bisque; detailed eyelashes and brows; mohair mustache and beard; cotton twill costume with fleece trim; turn-of-the-century.
MARKS: "8098//2/0" on back.
SEE: *Illustration 21. Shirley Karaba Collection.*

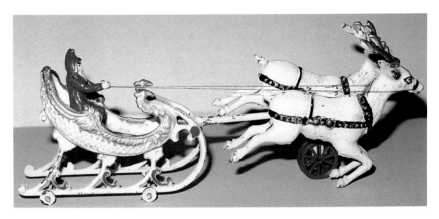

Hubley Santa in Sleigh: 18in (46cm) long; 7in (18cm) high; cast iron; early 20th century.

The wheels under the two reindeer give them the appearance of galloping. The Hubley Company was located in Lancaster, Pennsylvania. This toy is in unusually fine condition. **SEE:** *Illustration 22. David Bausch Collection.*

Cast Iron Santa and Advertising Card: 5in (13cm) 1904 green costume with long coat; cast iron Santa made at a later date.

The advertising card says, "L. Emery, Jr. & Co.// 43-45 Main Street// Bradford; Toy and Doll Bazar// Second Floor// Holiday Goods"; circa turn-of-the-century. **MARKS:** "1904" on base of cast iron Santa Claus. **SEE:** *Illustration 23.*

17

Santa Claus on Elephant (right): Pull-toy; papier-mâché elephant and Santa Claus; red felt coat and hat; blue felt pants; felt blanket; wheels inset in bottom of elephant's legs; head nods when pulled; turn-of-the-century.

Santa Claus on Donkey (left): Pull-toy; velvet over wood donkey; papier-mâché head, arms and boots on Santa; cloth body; faded red coat and hat; blue velvet pants; donkey has small wheels inserted into legs to make it roll; turn-of-the-century.

MARKS: None.

SEE: *Illustration 24. J. L. Roush Collection.*

Early Santa Claus: 12in (31cm); celluloid face; Germany; early 1900s.

This is the childhood doll of the owner's great grandfather which was in his office at Holly Mills (a flour mill) in West Texas.

SEE: *Illustration 25. Linda Yonker Collection.*

18

Chapter 2
Santa Claus
from 1911-1930

The 20th century brought many changes to western society, and the Santa Claus figures also changed. They took on a kinder look and were more often made with the shorter coat as pictured in the Thomas Nast drawings. The traditional materials of papier-mâché, wood, and glass began to give way to the new "composition" introduced to the United States by the E.I. Horsman Company. Celluloid was perfected for beautiful, inexpensive decorations. The character look was "in" for dolls and Santas, but not the "grouchy" look of the Belsnickle.

Many German toymakers had resettled in Pennsylvania and other locations in the United States, and their tin and cast iron mechanical Santas were elegant, whimsical and fun. From France came Père Noël candy box figures. Japanese manufacturers began to imitate the papier-mâché and celluloid German Santas during World War I, as German importation had ceased.

The 1920s "roared" with energy, verve and daring. The new Santa Clauses from this time reflected many of these trends.

Santa Sitting on Moss-covered Cornucopia:
7½in (19cm); papier-mâché Santa; short red flannel coat; blue flannel pants; painted, molded boots; sits on dried moss-covered cornucopia; probably German; circa 1910-1917.
SEE: *Illustration 26. Jane Anderson Collection.*

Up, Up, and Away in a Beautiful Balloon: 12in (31cm); tin balloon with pink Santa Claus in the basket; colors of the balloon are pink, blue, and white; 1970s reproduction of 1920s model. **SEE:** *Illustration 27. David Bausch Collection.*

Belsnickle Candy Container: 3in (8cm) by 4in (10cm) papier-mâché face; stuffed body on wire armature; flannel long tunic costume; painted molded papier-mâché shoes; paper beard and mustache; wooden sled; cardboard box with two types of fancy paper covering the top and bottom; 1910-1920.

This tiny old German Santa brought his candy and gifts in the time-honored tradition, but he dreamed of flying in the "new-fangled" inventions.

MARKS: "Germany" underside of sled.
SEE: *Illustration 27.*

Small Santa with Wood Basket on Back: 6in (15cm); papier-mâché ; small bell tinkles gently; long Santa robe; 1900-1920
MARKS: "Germany" on base.
SEE: *Illustration 29. David Bausch Collection.*

Large German Nodder Santa: 32in (81cm); papier-mâché head, boots; clay hands; stuffed body on armature; long flannel Santa robe with white flannel strip down the front; fur beard; carries large goose feather tree with ornaments; wood-slat basket; key-wind clockwork nodder; 1900-1917.

This was probably a store display.
SEE: *Illustration 28. Robert M. Merch Collection.*
Pressed Paper Santa: 16in (41cm); Santa ringing bell with left hand; carries pack over left shoulder (cannot be seen); red Santa coat and pants; white paper trim gives illusion of fur; store display; 1930s.

This Santa can be seen behind the large German nodder.
SEE: *Illustration 28. Robert M. Merch Collection.*

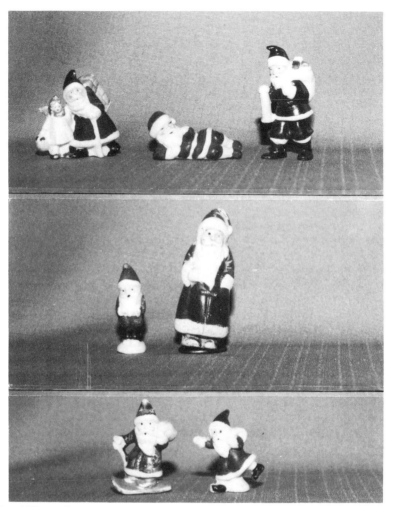

Painted Bisque Santas (Top row, left to right):
Santa with Angel: 1¾in by 1⅞in (5cm by 5cm); painted bisque.
MARKS: "7/60."
Sleeping Santa: 1in (3cm) by 2in (5cm); painted bisque.
MARKS: "GERMANY" incised in bisque.
Santa with Lantern: 2⅜in (6cm); painted bisque.
MARKS: "GERMANY" incised in bisque.
   These small figures were made during various time periods.

(Middle row, left to right):
Painted bisque Santa: 1⅞in (5cm).
MARKS: "JAPAN."
Painted bisque Santa: 3⅛in (8cm).
MARKS: "JAPAN."
(Bottom row, left to right):
Santa on Skis: painted bisque; 2in (5cm).
MARKS: "Japan S1185" incised in bisque.
Skating Santa: painted bisque; 1¾in (4cm).
MARKS: "JAPAN."
SEE: *Illustration 30A. Carole Correll Collection.*

Bisque Nodder: 2⅝in (7cm); painted bisque; circa 1920s. **MARKS:** "Germany." **SEE:** *Illustration 30B. Carole Correll Collection.*

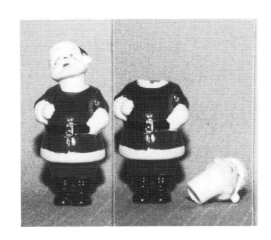

Chalk Belsnickle: 14½in (37cm); white, chalk-like plaster with brown paint brushed lightly over figure; sad look on face; brown Christmas tree; circa 1920s.

Plaster was a popular choice of material for Santas during much of the first half of the 20th century. Although they were widely made, collectors may have difficulty finding them because they were easily broken.

SEE: *Illustration 31. Jane Anderson Collection.*

Schoenhut Display Santa Claus: 15½in (39cm); unusual wood head and face not seen on other Schoenhut dolls; traditional Schoenhut body; hooks for reins in hands; hole for his pipe; his shoes have been replaced with old Schoenhut shoes; new mohair wig; original beard; original clothes; 1914.

This doll was accompanied by an advertisement that said, "Made to order only for store and window decorations." This doll also has a sleigh, Christmas tree, burlap sack and four wooden carved reindeer. The entire display is 5ft (152cm).
SEE: Illustration 32. Rosalie Whyel Museum of Doll Art, Bellevue, Washington. Photography by Charles Backus.

Santa in Moss-covered Sleigh: Complete toy is 13½in (34cm) long; 6in (15cm) high on wheeled platform; moss-covered sleigh; papier-mâché Santa dressed in a long red flannel robe; papier-mâché reindeer; circa 1910-1917.

This is an excellent example of a hard-to-find wheeled pull-toy.
SEE: *Illustration 33. Jane Anderson Collection.*

Santa Driving Moss-covered Car: 5in (13cm) long and 5½in (14cm) high; Santa wears a red flannel coat; blue flannel pants; black painted boots; small red velvet pillow glued to back of car; another red velvet pillow is behind Santa's back; 1910-1920.
SEE: *Illustration 34. Jane Anderson Collection.*

Belsnickle Sitting on Log: 6in (15cm) by 6in (15cm); bisque face; crepe paper clothing trimmed with cotton batting; cardboard log candy container; carries sticks and toy pack; German; circa 1910-1920.

The Germans often used wood in their Christmas figures. They revered their wooded landscape, and they tried to include it in their exports.

SEE: *Illustration 35. Jane Anderson Collection.*

Composition Santa Claus: 13in (33cm); unusually large, painted eyebrows; dressed in red flannel coat trimmed with white flannel; cotton batting beard; Germany; 1910-1920.

SEE: *Illustration 36. Jane Anderson Collection.*

26

Hubley Santa: 3in (8cm); painted cast iron; carrying packages; made in Lancaster, Pennsylvania; 1911-1930s.

The early cast iron Santas have a smooth finish because they were tumbled with sand in vats. The later Santas have a much rougher finish.

SEE: *Illustration 37. David Bausch Collection.*

Candy Container Santas: Papier-mâché; rabbit fur beards; hats and jackets are red flannel; the two small sizes are rare; 1920s. (Sizes from left to right: 10in [25cm]; 4¾in [12cm]; 15in [38cm]; 6½in [17cm]; 11½in [29cm].)

MARKS: "Germany."

SEE: *Illustration 38. Jane Anderson Collection.*

27

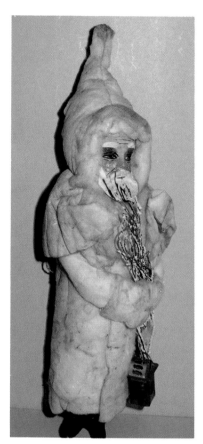

Père Noël: 12in (31cm); papier-mâché face; rolled cardboard candy container; white wadding clothes; carries switches; early electrically lighted lantern; French; 1911-1920s.
SEE: *Illustration 39. Phyllis S. Bechtold Collection.*

Two Belsnickles on a Pile of Logs: 6in (15cm) doll on left; 4in (10cm) doll on right; both are papier-mâché ; rabbit fur beards; dressed in flannel robes; candy boxes; probably German; 1900-1910.
Nodder on Donkey: 9in (23cm); papier-mâché; short red flannel jacket; blue flannel pants; black painted boots; sitting on a fiber-covered donkey; 1920s.
SEE: *Illustration 40. Jane Anderson Collection.*

Large Cloth Santa Claus:
18½in (47cm); mask face with fierce expression; cloth body; flannel costume with fur trim; early 1920s.
Early Belsnickle (hanging at waist): 3in (8cm); papier-mâché; gold paint with mica; 1890-1910.
Small Santa (hanging from right arm): 5in (13cm) papier-mâché; excellent details on face; flannel costume; unusual high pointed hat; early 1900s.
SEE: *Illustration 41. Mary Ann Hall Collection.*

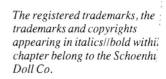

The registered trademarks, the trademarks and copyrights appearing in italics//bold within chapter belong to the Schoenhut Doll Co.

Schoenhut Roly Poly: 11½in (29cm); papier-mâché; painted features; early part of 20th century. **SEE:** *Illustration 42. De Fina Auctions.*

Bisque Santa: 9in (23cm); composition body and hands; red flannel costume; fur beard; goose feather tree with yarn woven into it for decorations; 1910-1920s.
SEE: *Illustration 43. David Bausch Collection.*

tmas with Porcelain
(25cm); papier-mâché face;
tume; brass basket on back;
carries green walking stick;
tury.
res seen in the picture are
attached to a battery. When the switch is
turned on, the candles light.
SEE: *Illustration 44. De Fina Auctions.*

30

Santa on Skis: 3in (8cm); cast metal Santa; metal skis and ski poles; 1920s-1930s.
MARKS: "Made in U.S.A."
SEE: *Illustration 45. Phyllis S. Bechtold Collection.*

Cast Iron Santa Clauses: 3in (8cm) to 6in (15cm); originally these Santa Clauses were painted bright colors. Most of the paint is gone. Cast iron figures were made from the 1880s to the 1930s.
SEE: *Illustration 46. Jean Hagerty Collection.*

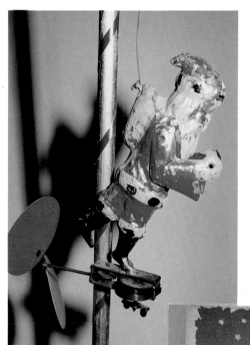

Flying Santa Claus: 7in (18cm); apparatus 2in (5cm); circa 1910-1920.

Flying Santa Clauses were very popular after 1910 when the *St. Nicholas Magazine* published an illustration of Santa flying in an airplane. Santa came also by dirigibles, zeppelins and balloons. Science fiction visionaries even made this self-propelled Santa. **SEE:** *Illustration 47. David Bausch Collection.*

Post Card of Santa in a Dirigible: This patriotic postcard of Santa looking down on the North American continent was mailed from Indianapolis, Indiana on December 24 at 3 P.M., 1909.

This type of flying Santa was a very popular Christmas tree decoration during the early part of the 20th century. **SEE:** *Illustration 48.*

Cloth Santa: 26in (66cm); all-cloth with mask face; mohair wig; satin Santa suit with black and white belt; mitten hands; American; 1920s. At left: Armand Marseille No. 370: Bisque head; ball-jointed body; long dark curls; all-original; long brown printed jumper; organdy blouse; straw hat with black feathers; 1910-1920.
MARKS: "Germany//370// A.O.M." on doll; none on Santa.
SEE: *Illustration 49.*

Large Candy Container: 19in (48cm); plaster over papier-mâché face, hands, boots; rabbit fur beard; flannel suit with chenille trim; oilcloth belt; goose feather tree; red lines around eyes and on forehead to intensify facial expression; 1920s.
MARKS: "Made in Germany" on seal on right foot.
SEE: *Illustration 50.*

Santa Claus with Fish Net Sack: 19in (48cm); cloth body; oilcloth hands; imitation fur beard, hair, and trim on costume; short red velvet coat; yellow velvet pants; broad legs and boots; 1920s into the 1930s.
SEE: *Illustration 51. Mary Ann Hall Collection.*

Santa in Car Candy Container: 6in (15cm) long; 5in (13cm) high; celluloid-type face; costume and candy container are netting; tin car with five stars; 1920s-1930s.
SEE: *Illustration 52. David Bausch Collection.*

The ₤ine Supreme is

G.E.M.
BRAND

ONDERFULLY
TRACTIVE

THOGRAPHED
HEAVY
ARD AND
LLED WITH
IE NICEST
TTLE TOYS
AT CAN BE
UND TO PLEASE
E LITTLE FOLKS

ERE IS NOTHING
IE QUITE SO
MPLETE ON THE
RKET

UR TOY DEPARTMENT
L NEED SOME

ufactured by the Producers of
E. M. BRAND
RISTMAS STOCKINGS
ESTABLISHED IN 1885

Santa Claus Filled with TOYS

25¢
50¢
$1.00

GEO. E. MOUSLEY, Inc.
2-04-06 RANSTEAD STREET   PHILADELPHIA, PA.

The registered trademarks, the trademarks and copyrights appearing in *italics//bold* within this chapter belong to *Geo. E. Mousley, Inc.*

Santa Claus Filled with Toys: This lithographed heavy cardboard Santa Claus was advertised in *Playthings Magazine* in January 1930. It was sold to retailers by Geo. E. Mousley, Inc.

During the 1930s drug stores, department stores, 5 and 10 cent stores, and even grocery stores sold heavy net Christmas stockings stuffed with inexpensive toys and candy. For many children this was an important part of the Santa Claus myth. This beautiful Santa Claus was a variation of this theme.
SEE: *Illustration 53. Playthings*, January 1930.

Santa with Electric Lantern: 13in (33cm); papier-mâché face and hands; flannel costume with blue pants; rabbit fur beard; goose feather tree; plaster base; a battery powers the electric lantern; circa late 1920s-1930s.
MARKS: "Japan" on base.
SEE: *Illustration 54. David Bausch Collection.*

The registered trademarks, the trademarks and copyrights appearing in italics//bold within this chapter belong to Ferdinand Strauss Corp.

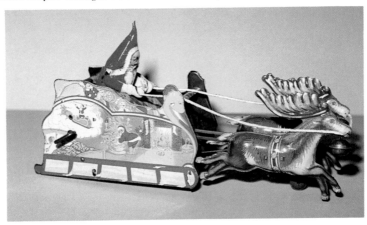

Tin Sleigh with Two Reindeer: 11in (28cm) long; 5in (13cm) high; wind-up toy; lithographed sled; 1923.

When the toy is wound-up, the reindeer give the appearance of galloping.

MARKS: "Santee Claus//Strauss Mechanical Toys//Known the World Over//Reg. U.S. Pat. Off.//Ferdinand Strauss Corp.//New York U.S.A.//U.S. Pat. October 18, 1921//U.S. Pat. December 11, 1923."

SEE: *Illustration 55. David Bausch Collection.*

The registered trademarks, the trademarks and copyrights appearing in italics//bold within this chapter belong to Willitts Designs.

On December 4, 1926 a Norman Rockwell painting appeared on the cover of *The Saturday Evening Post.* It showed Santa with a globe plotting his journey around the world. In 1988 a music box was made based on this painting.

In December 1931, *The Ladies' Home Journal* published the Christmas edition. The cover showed a beautiful little blonde girl crying as she wrote a letter to "Dear Santa."

It took a long time to get them together, but the picture and the music box symbolize the dreams that make the legend of Santa Claus a magical force in the world today.

Willitts Designs Music Box: all-ceramic; 6in (15cm) high; plays "Here Comes Santa Claus;" 1988.

SEE: *Illustration 56.*

These Candy Boxes are unusually fine examples of the French image of Père Noël. Their delicate pastel costumes of wadded cotton are fur trimmed. They carry either feather Christmas trees or a bundle of sticks. Their high facial coloring indicates they were made during the 1920s or 1930s. Each one is hand-painted with a different expression on the face.

Père Noël (doll on left): 6in (15cm); papier-mâché face mask; cardboard candy box body; wadding costume with mica sprinkles; goose feather tree.

Père Noël (doll in middle): 12in (31cm); three-piece carefully molded plaster face, beard and shoulders; (see *Illustration 58*); cardboard candy box body; lavender wadding cloth costume; goose feather tree.

Père Noël (doll on right): 7in (18cm); papier-mâché face mask; cardboard candy box body; yellow wadding costume trimmed in white; fur beard; bundle of sticks.

MARKS: None.

SEE: *Illustration 57* (dolls on left and right). *Margaret Benike Collection. Illustration 58* (doll in middle).

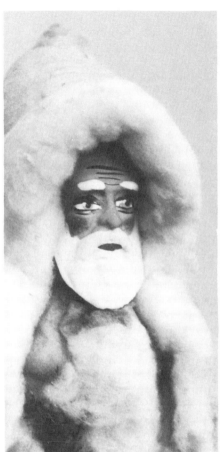

French Père Noël (closeup): for full-length picture see *Illustration 57*, (doll in middle).
MARKS: None.
SEE: *Illustration 58.*

French Père Noël (head only): unusual three-part plaster mold; 1¾in (5cm).
SEE: *Illustration 59.*

Store Display: Santa driving a sports car: F.M. Rudd Distributor; red Santa and red stars on car; 1930.
SEE: *Illustration 60. David Bausch Collection.*

Chapter 3

Santa Claus
from 1931-1950

After the 1929 crash of the stock market the world changed again and the opulent Christmas figures of the 1920s gave way to less expensive Santa Claus dolls and ornaments. Inexpensive papier-mâché and cardboard materials continued to be used, and the composition was a cheaper grade. Celluloid and glass toys from Japan were purchased more often than the more expensive European Christmas decorations.

By the middle of the 1930s, few metal toys were made in the United States as metal was in short supply. Santas were made of rubber until that, too, was forbidden for toy manufacture as World War II approached.

During World War II, Christmas continued to be celebrated with substitute materials and homemade decorations. It is unusual to find many Christmas collectibles from this period.

After the war, a new substance, called hard plastic, was introduced for dolls and toys. It was a wonderful substitute for flammable celluloid, and thousands of Christmas Santas and other decorations were made of this medium. They are still very bright and colorful. Because they are much sturdier than the early Christmas decorations more survived and they are more available for collectors.

Immediately after World War II, the Japanese made inexpensive celluloid and papier-mâché ornaments again, imprinted with "Made in Occupied Japan." There are not too many of these available today because the Japanese quickly turned to heavier industry and low priced ornaments were imported from other sources in the Orient.

A few "Made in Western Germany" Santas and Christmas decorations were also made. They are much more difficult to find.

By 1950 the production of Christmas "art" had returned to its prewar levels.

Santa Taking Off From North Pole: 9in (23cm) long; celluloid; reindeer pulling sled; unusual molding and colors; 1930s.
MARKS: "Made//in U.S.A."
SEE: *Illustration 61.*

Japanese Sleigh and Santa: 1930s; 5in (13cm) wide; 4in (10cm) tall; flocked papier-mâché sleigh; celluloid reindeer; red and white cotton batting Santa Claus trimmed with chenille; clay face, delicately painted with three lines on the forehead; 1930s.

Similar sleds and Santas were made in Germany and in the United States. Most of them have the country of origin stamped on the bottom of the sled.
MARKS: None.
SEE: *Illustration 62. Pat Parton Collection.*

**Japanese Santa Claus on
Sled:** 3½in (9cm) by 5in
(13cm); papier-mâché
head; wrapped chenille
over armature; wood sled;
carefully painted face;
1930s.
 This is a typical
oriental-looking Santa
Claus from Japan. He is
pictured in a typical
Japanese garden under a
Bonsai tree. In the
background is a small paper
house made in Japan. A
light bulb on a string of
Christmas tree lights could
be placed in a hole in the
back to let the light shine
through the window.
SEE: *Illustration 63.*

Santa Claus House: 4½in
(12cm); cardboard; painted and
mica scattered on house; made in
Japan. This type of Christmas tree
decoration was very popular in the
1930s. A light bulb from the string
of Christmas lights could be
inserted in the back, and the light
glowed through the simulated
stained glass window.
Santa Claus: 2in (8cm); painted
papier-mâché head; cotton body;
1930s.
SEE: *Illustration 64.*

Early Japanese Santa: 7in (18cm); papier-mâché face and hands; pre-World War II.

The early Japanese Christmas toys were excellent imitations of those made in Germany. After World War II, the quality of these toys deteriorated.
SEE: *Illustration 65. Phyllis S. Bechtold Collection.*

Chenille Santa Claus: 6½in (17cm); papier-mâché face; chenille arms and legs; flat body; dressed in rows of red chenille with mock fur trim; 1945-1948.

Chenille is a pipe cleaner-type material.
MARKS: "Made in Occupied Japan."
SEE: *Illustration 66. McMasters Productions.*

White Rotund Santa Claus: 9½in (25cm); molded, painted face and body; red trim; red net bag for toys; 1930s. **SEE:** *Illustration 67. McMasters Productions.*

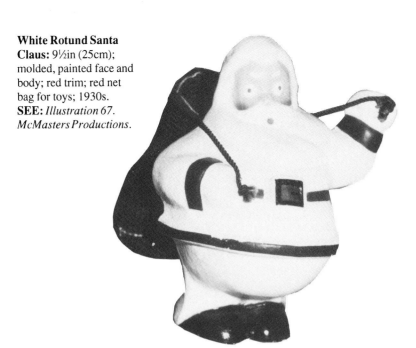

Chenille Santa Bell: 4in (10cm) high; pressed cardboard bell trimmed with paper chenille strips; papier-mâché head; cotton beard; 1930s. **SEE:** *Illustration 68. Joyce Barth.*

Fish Net Candy Container Santa Claus: 5½in (14cm); celluloid face and hands; fishnet costume with velvet-like arms and hat trimmed with fur; rafia chenille basket with paper holly leaf; Japanese; 1930s.

There were many Santa Clauses and other Christmas ornaments which used the netting in their construction. Some of them are delightful and unique.
SEE: *Illustration 69. Mary Ann Hall Collection.*

Celluloid Santas: (from left to right); 1930s.
1. 4in (10cm)
2. 8¾in (22cm).
3. 3½in (9cm).
4. 6in (15cm); lantern in left hand; Japan.
SEE: *Illustration 70. Jane Anderson Collection.*

Composition Santa Claus:
17½in (45cm); all-composition including molded hat; painted face; flannel costume with fake fur trim; black ribbed socks; red flannel bag; all-original; late 1920s-1930s.
MARKS: None.
SEE: *Illustration 71. McMasters Productions.*

The registered trademarks, the trademarks and copyrights appearing in italics// bold within this chapter belong to Irwin Toy Company.

Irwin Santas: Group of celluloid Santas; 2in (5cm) to 7in (18cm); 1930s.
MARKS: "Irwin USA." All have this mark.
SEE: *Illustration 72. Phyllis S. Bechtold Collection.*

Santa Claus with Walking Stick: 5½in (14cm); papier-mâché; painted white with mica sprinkled on suit; berry used for nose; metal walking stick; carrying a Christmas tree made from a large seal; red crepe paper hat with white trim; 1930s.
MARKS: "Made in Austria" stamped on bottom of left foot.
SEE: *Illustration 73.*

Japanese Santa: 11in (28cm); celluloid head; arms and legs are thin wire; cloth costume trimmed with fur; 1930s.
MARKS: "TY (inside diamond)" on paper label.
SEE: *Illustration 74.*
Phyllis S. Bechtold Collection.

German Nodder: 7in (18cm); papier-mâché; nodder mechanism is based on a wooden peg on a spring; red coat and hat; blue pants; late 1920s-1930s.
SEE: *Illustration 75* (doll on right). *David Bausch Collection.*
Mechanical Santa Ringing Bell: 6in (15cm); celluloid head; tin feet and body; cloth suit over metal body; neck is a bellows that allows the head to go up and down; Santa shakes bell; key wind; Japan; 1930s.
SEE: *Illustration 75* (doll on left). *Phyllis S. Bechtold Collection.*

Santa with Snap Hands: 9in (23cm); composition face with bulging enamel eyes; metal body; rayon Santa costume; fur collar; cotton trim; spring clip hands; red gloves; 1930s.

The spring hands have been holding Mr. Geppi's business cards for many years.
MARKS: None.
SEE: *Illustration 76. C.M. Geppi Collection.*

The registered trademarks, the trademarks and copyrights appearing in italics//bold within this chapter belong to C. Rempel Mfg. Inc.

Rubber Santa Claus: 11in (28cm); all-rubber; baby squeeze toy; large black gloves like boxer's gloves; 1930s.
MARKS: "C. Rempel Mfg. Inc.// Akron 11 Ohio U.S.A."
SEE: *Illustration 77.*

Santa Claus Candy Container: 9in (23cm); pressed cardboard (resembles old egg cartons); costume painted red and white; mica scattered over paint; 1930s.
MARKS: "Pat.//Appld//For" on bottom of left foot.
SEE: *Illustration 78.*

German Santa with Packages: 10in (25cm); painted cloth face with excellent details; flannel Santa Costume; carrying packages.
MARKS: ".....DART" on yellow label that can be seen at the bottom of coat.
SEE: *Illustration 79. David Bausch Collection.*

Wobbly Head Santa Bank: 8in (20cm);
composition; fur beard; head nods and
wobbles; bell rings; 1930s-1950s.
MARKS: "For Xmas" on stomach; "Estra//
Germany" on base.
SEE: *Illustration 80* (doll on left). *Phyllis S.
Bechtold Collection.*
Old Fashion Santa Claus: 7½in (19cm);
composition face; fur beard; red flannel robe
and hat; blue flannel skirt; 1940s.
MARKS: "Germany."
SEE: *Illustration 80* (doll on right). *Jane
Anderson Collection.*

Grinning Santa with Doll in Back Pack:
14½in (37cm); all-composition; red flannel
coat and hat; basket on back; blue painted
hands; black boots with white "snow" painted
on them; circa 1930s.
SEE: *Illustration 81. Jane Anderson
Collection.*

Head Moving Santa: 7in (18cm); celluloid; had weighted mechanism which moves the head; tin base.

Doll is pictured showing the front and the back.

MARKS: "J.F.E.C.T.M.A. Inspection Passed" on red and white paper sticker; "K (inside bell)" impressed on doll.

SEE: *Illustration 82. Phyllis S. Bechtold Collection.*

Candy Container: 9¼in (24cm); papier-mâché; fur beard, hat and coat are flocked; coat trimmed in chenille; late 1940s.

MARKS: "Made in West Germany."

SEE: *Illustration 83. Jane Anderson Collection.*

Electric Glass Santa: 8in (20cm); ceramic base.

SEE: *Illustration 84. David Bausch Collection.*

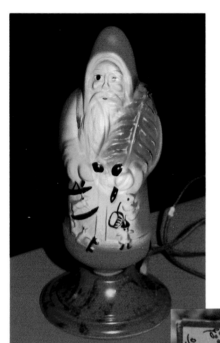

Belsnickle-type Lamp: 9in (23cm) glass; unusual colors of red, yellow, orange blended in costume; Bakelite bases; still working; 1930s.

Electric candles began to replace traditional candles in the 1930s. There were many variations of these electrified glass bulbs. Also lamp shades were painted with Santa Claus scenes.

MARKS: "Made in Japan" on base.
SEE: *Illustration 85. Chuck's Antiques of Medina, Ohio.*

ARTWOOD PRODUCTS

Jump Jump: 3½in (9cm); composition head; painted face; wire body; felt clothes; carries cloth candy cane; 1948.
MARKS: "Jump Jump// Holiday House//1948" on box.
SEE: *Illustration 86.*

The registered trademarks, the trademarks and copyrights appearing in italics//bold within this chapter belong to Rushton Company.

RUSHTON

Coca Cola®️ Santa Claus (doll on right): 16in (41cm); molded rubber face; plush body and hat; black leatherette hat; mock white fur trim and beard; rubber boots; carrying a miniature bottle of Coca Cola; 1940.
MARKS: "©//Rushton//Co." molded on boot.
SEE: *Illustration 87.*

DAKIN

Coca Cola Santa Claus (doll on left): 15½in (39cm); vinyl head and limbs; cloth body; red suit with black leatherette belt; plush trim; 1984.
MARKS: "Coca Cola Company" on tag; "R. Dakin & Co." on label.
SEE: *Illustration 87.*
 The Santa Claus figure went through another change in 1931 when Haddon Sundbloom produced his famous rendering of Santa Claus for a Coca Cola advertisement (background picture). This picture and the Coca Cola product have since spread around the world.
 In 1940 the Rushton Company of Atlanta, Georgia made a doll which was based on the original advertisement. There were other Rushton editions over the middle years of this century, including a black version. Dakin produced a 1980s version.

Early Japanese Santa Claus: 5in (13cm); composition face, hands and boots; blue cloth pants, felt jacket and cap; carries gold wire Christmas tree; face painted with red lines on forehead to make him look fierce; late 1920s-early 1930s.
SEE: *Illustration 88. Wallace C. Judd Family Collection.*

Felt Santa Claus: 10in (25cm); felt body; unusual face with seam across the face and up each side of nose; glass eyes; individual fingers; red felt Santa costume with fur trim; black felt boots; 1930s.

This is a Steiff look-alike.
MARKS: Black octagon button with gold rim; "R" in middle of button sewn on right hand.
SEE: *Illustration 89. Margaret Benike Collection.*

Group of Japanese Santa Clauses: These dolls were made in the 1930s and again in the late 1940s. The dolls of the 1930s were better made than the ones after World War II. (See *Illustration 98.*)
MARKS: "Occupied Japan" or "Japan."
SEE: *Illustration 90. Phyllis S. Bechtold Collection.*

Japanese Santa Claus: 16in (41cm); papier-mâché; 1930s.
SEE: *Illustration 91. Linda Yonker Collection.*

Japanese Santa with Stick: 10¼in (26cm); painted composition face; flannel coat; cotton pants; cotton batting beard; coat is trimmed with thin band of fur; black boots; white stand with mica flakes sprinkled up over boots to indicate snow; 1930-1935.
MARKS: "Japan" on stand.
SEE: *Illustration 92. Jane Anderson Collection.*

The registered trademarks, the trademarks and copyrights appearing in italics//bold within this chapter belong to the Gund Mfg. Co.

GUND MFG. CO.

Gund Musical Santa Claus: 16in (41cm); all-cloth with stiffened mask face; corduroy stuffed body; plush beard and trim on hood; music box plays "Jingle Bells;" bells on coat instead of buttons; 1940s. **MARKS:** "Gund Mfg. Co.//(J. Swedline Inc. SUCC.)//200-5th Ave. N.Y.C. 10, N.Y." on tag sewn into Santa costume.
SEE: *Illustration 93*.

Clockwork Head Nodder Santa Claus: 16in (41cm); composition head; glass eyes; store display; late 1940s. **MARKS:** "U.S. Zone// Germany."
SEE: *Illustration 94. C. Gordon Hitchings Collection.*

Chapter 4
Santa Claus
from 1951-1970

After World War II, the manufacturers of dolls and toys quickly turned to hard plastic to make them. Hard plastic had been developed as a war material. Millions of hard plastic dolls, figures, candy containers, and other Christmas decorations flooded the market. They were carefully molded and were very attractive. They did not break like ones of fragile materials from the past.

The Japanese continued to make Christmas decorations into the early 1950s. The traditional papier-mâché Santa Clauses were made, but their legs were of rolled paper, and the bodies leaned forward on their stands. Very soon the Japanese manufacturers turned to other more profitable products, and by the late 1950s, many of the Santa Claus items came from Mexico, Hong Kong, Taiwan, and countries in the Far East.

Hard plastic was an excellent but expensive material, and by 1957 many of the toy and doll companies were using vinyl for manufacture. So did the makers of Santa Clauses.

By 1970, wherever Santas were manufactured in the world, the children and parents of those countries learned about him and some enjoyed talking about "Christmas Old Man." Movies and television also helped spread his fame around the world.

In the United States during this time period, there was a growth of nostalgia for the "old" Santas, and collectors began to look for unique and beautiful ones from the past. Collectors today now realize that wonderful Santa Clauses were also made during the 1950s and 1960s. It is nice to know that Santa Claus does not get old and fade away, he just becomes more collectible.

Santa Claus Waving His Hand:
6in (15cm); papier-mâché,
molded in one-piece; flocked red
Santa Claus suit; fake fur trim;
white flocked boots; 1950s.
MARKS: None.
SEE: *Illustration 96. McMasters*
Productions.

COLUMBIA TOY PRODUCTS

The registered trademarks, the trademarks and
copyrights appearing in italics//bold within this
chapter belong to Columbia Toy Products.

Harold Gale Line of Santas: Ideal for window and store displays; hand painted, life-like
facial features; made of red velveteen with plush trim; all Santas operate on electricity;
1962.

#1800 Animated Santa Claus (upper row left): 5ft, 5in (168cm); motorized; right arm
moves up and down; body swings from side to side.

#120 Stationary Santa Claus (upper row right): 14in (36cm).

#1813 Animated Santa in Boot (lower row far left): Motorized Santa with rotating
movement; 24in (61cm).

#1812 Animated Santa Claus in Chimney (lower row second left): Motorized Santa
with rotating movement; 25in (64cm).

#1808 Stationary Santa on Ball (lower row second right): 20in (51cm); mounted on
snowflake glitter ball.

#1801 Animated Santa Claus (lower row far right): Motorized Santa Claus; head turns;
arms move up and down.

MARKS: "Columbia Toy Products//Kansas City, 27, Mo."
SEE: *Illustration 95. Playthings,* March 1952.

Ornaments that are illuminated have been part of the Christmas and Santa Claus tradition for many years. These 1950s Santas each have a hole in their back that can be used to insert a small light bulb and cord.

Lighted Santas (from left to right):

1. 9in (23cm); enamel and flocked paint over metal; molded face with unusual eyebrow treatment; upper torso only; made by Glo Light Corporation of Chicago; 1950s.
MARKS: None.
SEE: *Illustration 97. Wallace C. Judd Family Collection.*

2. 16½in (42cm); entire doll is molded hard plastic; well-sculpted facial features; 1950s.
MARKS: None.
SEE: *Illustration 97. Wallace C. Judd Family Collection.*

3. 7½in (19cm); molded hard plastic; can be used as a candle holder or lamp; 1950s.
MARKS: None.
SEE: *Illustration 97. Wallace C. Judd Family Collection.*

Post World War II Santa Claus: 4in (10cm); papier-mâché mask face; cardboard body; red flannel Santa suit; blue rolled paper legs; cardboard base; white chenille trim on suit; pipe cleaner hands; bottle brush tree; 1950s.

Even at this late date, the Japanese Santas were still painted with German character faces with red lines on the foreheads of these inexpensive dolls. **MARKS:** "Japan" printed on base. **SEE:** *Illustration 98.*

Magge Head Kane Santa Claus and the Pixie Book: 19in (48cm); molded "Masse" head, arms, legs; cloth body; red velvet suit with mock fur; 1953.

"Masse" is a special type of composition used by the sculptor.

An original Pixie book and record by Magge Head Kane came with the doll. **MARKS:** "M Head (heart)" on back. **SEE:** *Illustration 99.*

Group of Hard Plastic Santa Clauses (left to right):
1. 3in (8cm); when his base is pushed down, the whole body moves as if he is saying "Ho Ho."
2. 4in (10cm); fur beard and trim on bottom of coat.
3. 3½in (9cm); Santa in sleigh.
4. 4in (10cm); tree ornament.
5. 3½in (9cm); candy container.
SEE: *Illustration 100A. Phyllis S. Bechtold Collection.*

Howdy Doody and Santa Claus Illuminated Wall Plaque: 10in by 13in (25cm by 33cm); embossed and painted on plastic-coated paper; mid-1950s.
MARKS: "© Kagram// Royal Electric Company, Inc."
SEE: *Illustration 100B. Wallace C. Judd Family Collection.*

KIDDIE PRODUCTS, INC.

The registered trademarks, the trademarks and copyrights appearing in italics//bold within this chapter belong to Kiddie Products, Inc.

Roly-Poly Santas: Dolls on Right and Left: 4½in (12cm); hard plastic; bells chime when rolling; red costume with yellow toy pack; shown front and back; 1950s. Doll in Middle: 4½in (12cm); hard plastic; bells chime when rolling; similar doll but has beautiful scalloped beard; 1950s. **MARKS:** "Kiddie Products.Avon,Mass." (dolls on right and left); "Fun World, Inc. N.Y. N.Y." (doll in middle). **SEE:** *Illustration 101. Phyllis S. Bechtold Collection.*

The registered trademarks, the trademarks and copyrights appearing in italics//bold within this chapter belong to Bradford.

A Winter Scene: 4in (10cm); hard plastic Santa and reindeer; styrofoam base and candle; wire Christmas tree; 1950s. **MARKS:** "A//Winter//Scene//by//Bradford" on box. **SEE:** *Illustration 102. Shirley Karaba Collection.*

Lead Santa: 3in (8cm) painted lead; early Santa costume; Santa carries a fan.
SEE: *Illustration 103.*
David Bausch Collection.

Santa Claus with Green Gloves: 8in (20cm); molded rubber squeak toy; 1957.
MARKS: "Made in U.S.A.//1957."
SEE: *Illustration 104.*
Jane Anderson Collection.

Climbing Santa Candy Container: 10in (25cm); glass stick container; filled with traditional Christmas candies; lever moves hard plastic Santa up and down on the container; 1960s.

These novelties were given as Christmas presents by the owner to her elementary class in the 1960s.
SEE: *Illustration 105.*
Mary Ann Hall Collection.

Three Hard Plastic Santas (from left to right): 1950s-early 1960s.
Santa on Reindeer: 6in by 6½in (15cm by 17cm); nicely molded Santa with flowing beard on galloping reindeer.
Santa standing in Sleigh: 3in by 3½in (8cm by 9cm); white sleigh candy container; red Santa.
Santa on Reindeer: 3in by 3½in (8cm by 9cm); smaller version of Santa on left.
MARKS: None.
SEE: *Illustration 106.*

The registered trademarks, the trademarks and copyrights appearing in italics//bold within this chapter belong to Harett-Gilmar, Inc.

Santa Claus Lamp: 7in (18cm); molded hard plastic; crown on head; holds mica-covered star; late 1950s-early 1960s.
MARKS: "Harett-Gilmar, Inc." molded on bottom of stand.
SEE: *Illustration 107.*

Mechanical Santa: 72in (182cm); life-size; celluloid face; Santa costume over framework; moves from side to side; store display; 1950s.
SEE: *Illustration 108. C. Gordon Hitchings Collection.*

Spring Push Toy: 4½in (12cm); spinning Christmas tree opens to show a Santa on the inside; action controlled by push spring, 1950s.
SEE: *Illustration 109. Shirley Karaba Collection.*

The registered trademarks, the trademarks and copyrights appearing in italics//bold within this chapter belong to Georgene Averill Dolls.

Averill Kris Kringle: 11in (28cm); vinyl face; cloth body; very curly mock-fur beard; red and white flannel Santa suit and cap; leatherette belt with silver buckle; black leatherette shoes; bell on end of pointed cap and on front of doll; white wool scarf; late 1950s-early 1960s.
MARKS: None on doll; "Kris Kringle//A Georgene Doll" on tag and box.
SEE: *Illustration 110.*

Bisque Santa Clauses (from left to right): Faces and costumes painted.
1. 3½in (9cm); long, flowing beard; long red robe with white trim.
2. 2¼in (6cm); short red and white coat with yellow painted belt; blue pants.
3. 4in (10cm); entire costume is red and white; carries yellow bag over shoulder.
4. 3in (8cm); short red and white coat; blue pants; molded to appear to be laughing.
MARKS: Some are marked "Germany;" the others are marked "Japan."
SEE: *Illustration 111. Jane Anderson Collection.*

Roly Poly Santa: 9in (23cm); molded hard plastic child's toy; 1960s.
MARKS: None.
SEE: *Illustration 112. Wallace C. Judd Family Collection.*

The registered trademarks, the trademarks and copyrights appearing in italics//bold within this chapter belong to Walt Disney Productions.

Mickey Mouse Lamp: 15in (38cm); molded rigid vinyl; 1960s.
  Lightbulb is inserted in hole in back of figure.
MARKS: "Walt Disney Productions//Made in USA-024276/1560" molded in vinyl on back.
SEE: *Illustration 113.*

Hard Plastic Santa Clauses:
5in (13cm); all three Santas are
from the same mold — pull-
toy, standing Santa, Santa in
sleigh candy container; 1950s.
MARKS: None.
SEE: *Illustration 114. Wallace
C. Judd Family Collection.*

Knickerbocker
Toy Company, Inc.

*The registered trademarks, the
trademarks and copyrights
appearing in italics//bold
within this chapter belong to
Knickerbocker Toy Company,
Inc.*

Baby Santa: 11½in (29cm);
vinyl head; plush body and
limbs; tiny beard, mustache
and arched eyebrows; white
felt hands; 1955.
MARKS: "Knickerbocker//
Toy Company, Inc.//New York
U.S.A." on tag sewn into body.
SEE: *Illustration 115.*

Cycle Santa: 5in (13cm); early vinyl; tin tricycle brightly painted; wind-up toy; bell attached to ring as Santa rides; early 1950s.
MARKS: "Made in Japan" on head of Santa.
SEE: *Illustration 116.*

Plastic Friction Toy: 5in (13cm); very hard plastic Santa, early vinyl base; 1950s.
MARKS: "Made in Japan" on base.
SEE: *Illustration 117. Phyllis S. Bechtold Collection.*

Santa in Tin Sleigh: 8in (20cm) long by 3½in (9cm) high; celluloid Santa and reindeer; green tin sled; 1950s.

This is a push-toy. When the sled is pushed, a bell rings.
MARKS: "Made in Japan" on bottom of sled.
SEE: *Illustration 118. Joyce W. Barth.*

Pop-up Santa in Chimney: 3in (8cm); hard plastic chimney; hard vinyl Santa face; early 1960s.

Face pops up when lid is opened.
MARKS: None.
SEE: *Illustration 119.*

Belsnickle-type: 19in (48cm); molded, painted hollow plaster; ruddy cheeks; long red and white robe; carries old goose feather tree; toys are early papier-mâché; teddy bear is jointed.

It is difficult to determine the age of this figure. Molded hollow plaster Santas were made for many years. Because of the high color it has probably been made after World War II.
SEE: *Illustration 120. Mary Ann Hall Collection.*

Sleeping Santa Claus Candy Container: 8in (20cm); cardboard.
SEE: *Illustration 121A. Linda Yonker Collection.*

Whitman's Santa and Sleigh Candy Container: 11in (28cm) long; sleigh and deer are made of 1/4in (.65cm) sturdy printed cardboard; the colors include red, yellow, blue, brown, and pink.
MARKS: "Merry//Christmas//Whitman's" on sleigh.
SEE: *Illustration 121B. De Fina Auctions.*

The registered trademarks, the trademarks and copyrights appearing in italics//bold within this chapter belong to Steiff.

Steiff Santa Claus: 4½in (12cm); rubber-like latex head and hands; felt body and costume; plush trim and beard; Steiff button attaches label to coat.

This is a hard-to-find small Steiff Santa Claus. Other sizes were 8in (20cm) and 11in (28cm). These dolls were made for several years. Steiff made a reproduction 11in (28cm) Santa Claus in the early 1980s. (See *Illustration 122*). The chest tag has the word "Reproduction" on it.

MARKS: "Steiff (cursive)" button under coat.
"Steiff Original Marke//Santa Claus//(picture of bear)" on chest tag.
"Steiff//Original//113//Made in//Germany" on yellow tag.
SEE: *Illustration 122*.

Woolworth Co.

The registered trademarks, the trademarks and copyrights appearing in italics//bold within this chapter belong to F.W. Woolworth Co

Climb the Roof, Musical Santa: 9in (23cm); styrofoam house and sleigh; vinyl Santa and reindeer; 1960s.

Instructions say, "Pull out Santa from chimney and stand on edge of roof and watch him walk back into the chimney."

While he is climbing the roof, the music box plays "Jingle Bells."

MARKS: "Factory No. 1005//Item No. 1005/760//Dist. by F.W. Woolworth Co., New York, N.Y. 10007//Made in Japan."
SEE: *Illustration 123*.

Plush and Vinyl Santa
(doll on left): 20in (51cm);
plump vinyl face; body and
pointed cap are red and
white plush; fur-type beard;
1960s.

Plush and Vinyl Santa
(doll on right): 17in (43cm);
narrow face; body and
pointed cap are red and
white plush; fur-type beard;
1960s.

These Santas were sold
as children's toys and also to
merchants and display
people as advertising or
display items. The same
type of doll can be found
with many different faces.
MARKS: None.
SEE: *Illustration 124.*
Wallace C. Judd Family
Collection.

Wadding Santas: 7in (18cm); white wadding body; 1950s-type
Santa seals for faces; mica trim on doll at right; 1950s.
SEE: *Illustration 125. Shirley Karaba Collection.*

Spinning Toy Santa (right): 4in (10cm); hard plastic; top pops off when twisted; 1961-1980.
SEE: *Illustration 126. Phyllis S. Bechtold Collection.*
Santa House Bank: 4in (10cm); hard plastic; when coins are dropped in the roof, Santa comes out the chimney.
SEE: *Illustration 126. Phyllis S. Bechtold Collection.*

Pine Cone Elves: 3in (8cm); molded hard vinyl heads; pine cone bodies; papier-mâché feet (elves on right have pipe cleaner legs); cardboard base covered with mica; holding (from left to right) ornaments, package, stocking and Christmas tree; 1950s.

Pine cones were used as a material for Christmas decorations during the 19th century. (See *Illustration 3.*) They are still popular today.
MARKS: "Japan" printed on base.
SEE: *Illustration 127. Pat Parton Collection.*

Musical Carousel: 12½in (32cm); styrofoam carousel; vinyl deer and Santa Claus; Santa costume is flocked on the vinyl; top circle can be wound to start music; plays "Jingle Bells;" early 1960s.
MARKS: None.
SEE: *Illustration 128.*

The registered trademarks, the trademarks and copyrights appearing in italics//bold within this chapter belong to Holiday Fair, © Hedayas & Co. Holiday Ltd.

Holiday Fair (Canada)

Canadian Santa Claus: 11in (28cm); vinyl head; red felt body; vinyl boots; leatherette belt with silver paper buckle; 1966.
MARKS: "Holiday Fair ©//Hedayas & Co. N.Y.C.//Holiday Ltd, Toronto// Made in Japan."
SEE: *Illustration 129. Wallace C. Judd Family Collection.*

Pink Santa Claus: 13½in (34cm); molded vinyl head, hands, boots; cloth body; pink and white flannel Santa costume with plush trim; mohair-type beard; 1960s.

This color pink was very popular in the 1960s. It is very similar to the pink color seen in recent years from Austria. **SEE:** *Illustration 130. Wallace C. Judd Family Collection.*

The registered trademarks, the trademarks and copyrights appearing in italics//bold within this chapter belong to H.D.I.//HTC.

HTC Japan

Santa Claus Bank: 11in (28cm); metal bank; Santa Claus has vinyl head; metal body; battery powered electric eyes; patent leather boots trimmed with bells; 1960.

When a coin is deposited in the chimney of the house, Santa Claus's eyes light up and his body moves and rings the metal bell in his hand. **MARKS:** "© 1960 N.D.I.//HTC// Japan" printed on bank. **SEE:** *Illustration 131.*

The registered trademarks, the trademarks and copyrights appearing in italics//bold within this chapter belong to Marx.

Marx

Walking Santa Claus: 3in (8cm); molded hard plastic; black feet attached to inside of body; made in Hong Kong; 1950s.

When the Santa Claus is placed on a slight incline, he "walks" down the ramp smiling all the way.

MARKS: "Marx (over an X)" molded into plastic on yellow bag.

SEE: *Illustration 132. Pat Parton Collection.*

Troll Santa (doll on right): 8in (20cm); vinyl; flannel Santa costume; orange button-type eyes; hair implanted in head; 1950s.

Originally made in Sweden, Trolls were later made in the United States.

Santa Mask (left): This mask was made for a Belsnickle costume in the early part of the 20th century. The entire costume including the hat is made of bright red cotton. The mask has the "fierce" look of the Belsnickle, and the costume has a long, slim coat.

SEE: *Illustration 133. Helen Marlowe Collection* (troll).

Santa's Elf: 3½in (9cm); papier-mâché ; painted face; wadding beard; costumed painted gray and sprinkled with mica; 1930s.
MARKS: "Made in Japan."
SEE: *Illustration 134.*

Wind-up Santa Copter (left): 5in (13cm); painted metal body; plastic propellers; wind-up key; early 1960s.
MARKS: "Made in Japan" on side of copter.
SEE: *Illustration 135.*
Pressed Cardboard Santa Claus Candy Container (right): 6½in (17cm) high; 8in (20cm) wide; painted and glazed; 1940s-1950s.
MARKS: None.
SEE: *Illustration 135.*

Chapter 5
Santa Claus from 1971 to the Present

Santa Claus has moved into the end of the 20th century, not as an antique, but as a living legend around the world. Even the most avid antique collector seems to have a few contemporary Santas.

Effanbee, Vogue, Annalee and many other doll companies have made Christmas specials. Hallmark and American Greetings produce new Santas as gifts for collectors.

Novelties still come from Hong Kong, China, Taiwan, Germany, England, France and many other countries. Walt Disney Enterprises continues to dress their traditional plush Mickey and Minnie Mouse as Santa and Mrs. Claus.

There have been some wonderful reproduction sets to collect. Faith Wick has designed Santas for Ashton-Drake, and Mary Moline has delighted us with her bisque dolls inspired by mid-century Norman Rockwell illustrations.

The most surprising trend from the North Pole is the return of the patriotic Santa. Versions of the turn-of-the-century red, white and blue Santas compete with modern geometric Santas.

All these contemporary dolls and figures of Santa can now be added to the collecting fun of future generations. I wonder what the next century will bring?

The registered trademarks, the trademarks and copyrights appearing in italics//bold within this chapter belong to SNP.

SNP Chicago, Illinois
Santa Claus and Mrs. Santa Claus in Electric Wreath: Rigid vinyl wreath with the heads only; lights up in circling pattern; 1973.
MARKS: "SNP//Chicago, Illinois" on back of head.
SEE: *Illustration 136. Shirley Karaba Collection.*

Santa Snow Scenes (left to right): 3in (8cm); 5½in (14cm); 2in (5cm); plastic scenes in plastic domes; the Santa in the middle is vinyl except for the scene; 1970s.
MARKS: "Made in Hong Kong" on base.
SEE: *Illustration 137.*

Pepsi Cola® Santa Claus: Hard vinyl face; red velvet costume covering body shaped with sponges; white vinyl belt and boots with heels; plush trim. In the early 1970s the Pepsi Cola distributor in the Cleveland area gave these Santa Clauses to customers for promotion purposes. Other Pepsi distributors may have given them also. Over the years, Pepsi Cola gave other Santa figures away at Christmas time.
UNUSUAL IDENTIFYING FEATURE: Sponge bodies.
MARKS: None.
SEE: *Illustration 138. Pat Parton Collection.*

*The registered trademarks,
the trademarks and
copyrights appearing in
italics//bold within this
chapter belong to Christie
Mfg. Co.*

Christie Mfg. Co.

Wizard Santa Claus: 13in
(33cm); felt face and hands;
cloth body and legs; plush
Santa costume; felt cutouts
for facial features; 1970s.
MARKS: "Christy Cutie//
Christie Mfg Company" on
cloth label.
SEE: *Illustration 139.*

Hallmark Santa Claus: 7in
(18cm); printed cloth;
Tudor-style house box;
1978.
MARKS: "Hallmark" on
bottom of box.
SEE: *Illustration 140. Jayne
Keller Collection.*

Carlson Dolls

American Santa Claus: 7in (18cm) hard plastic; sleep eyes; wine-colored Santa Claus costume; mock-fur trim; black leatherette shoes and belt; 1974.

The tag says, "A collector's item, not an ordinary toy. Manufactured with the founders of America in mind to keep Americans aware of their heritage."

The Carlson Doll Company made a large line of costumed dolls. They were inexpensive and often purchased at historical sites.

MARKS: "Carlson//Dolls//Santa Claus" on tag.

SEE: *Illustration 141.*

Hallmark Santas (from left to right): 6in (15cm), 7in (18cm), 4¾in (12cm); all printed cloth; 1976, 1978, 1980s.

SEE: *Illustration 142. Jayne Keller Collection.*

The registered trademarks, the trademarks and copyrights appearing in italics//bold within this chapter belong to American Greetings Corp.

American Greetings Corp.

American Greetings Corp. Santa: 2½in (6cm); printed cloth; 1982.

The green tag in the box says, "Wishing you all the joys of a good old-fashioned Christmas."

MARKS: "MCMLXXXII//American Greetings Corp.//Cleve.Ohio 44144//Made in Taiwan//XMSO-4" on cloth tag.

SEE: *Illustration 143.*

Kurt Adler, Inc.

Yo Yo Santa: 2in (5cm); metal; 1970s.
MARKS: "Kurt Adler, Inc. N.Y." on back.
SEE: *Illustration 143.*

The registered trademarks, the trademarks and copyrights appearing in italics//bold within this chapter belong to Florabelle Flowers, Inc.

Florabelle Flowers, Inc.

Santa's Sleigh: 6in by 13in (15cm by 33cm); vinyl sleigh, deer, Santa Claus, and presents; red sleigh and decorations on reindeer; red, yellow, and white packages; 1970s-1980s.
MARKS: "Florabelle Flowers, Inc." on tag.
SEE: *Illustration 144. Wallace C. Judd Family Collection.*

Ho Ho Ho Santa Clauses (left to right): 8in (20cm); 15in (38cm); small Santa is washcloth-type knit; large Santa is cut from cotton material by-the-yard; 1970s.

Both of these Santa Clauses are especially bright and cheerful although inexpensive when originally purchased.
MARKS: None.
SEE: *Illustration 145. Wallace C. Judd Family Collection.*

Applehead Santa: 10½in (27cm); apple head; cloth body; red velvet suit; felt hands; soft vinyl boots; 1970s.

This seems to be a commercial product rather than a homemade Santa.
MARKS: None.
SEE: *Illustration 146. Wallace C. Judd Family Collection.*

United Features Syndicate, Inc.

Snoopy Santa: 11½in (29cm); plush body; red and white flannel Santa costume; black vinyl belt with gold buckle; Snoopy copyright 1968; outfit and doll were made in the mid-1980s.

MARKS: "1968 United Features Syndicate, Inc.// Product of Korea" on tag sewn into body.

SEE: *Illustration 147.*

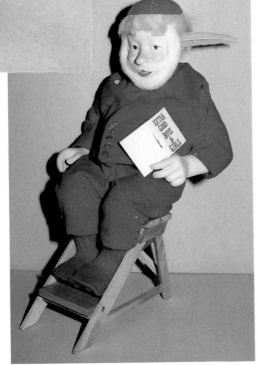

Santa by Mary Moline: 12in (31cm); bisque; unusual velvet Santa Claus leisure costume; character doll in the Norman Rockwell series; 1984.

This Santa was one of the first dolls in the series with the original beard. Problems caused them to change the beard later.

MARKS: Little car wrist tag.
SEE: *Illustration 148. Phyllis S Bechtold Collection.*

The registered trademarks, the trademarks and copyrights appearing in italics//bold within this chapter belong to Rumbleseat Dolls.

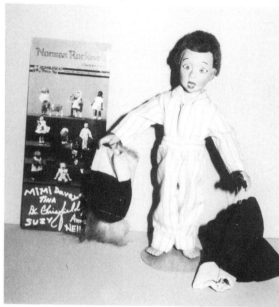

Rumbleseat Dolls

Davey: 9in (23cm); all-bisque; carries Santa bag, hat, and beard; by Mary Moline in her first Norman Rockwell Series; 1980. **Norman Rockwell Brochure:** *Davey* is pictured on the next-to-the top row on the right. **MARKS:** Little car wrist tag. **SEE:** *Illustration 149. Phyllis S. Bechtold Collection.*

The registered trademarks, the trademarks and copyrights appearing in italics//bold within this chapter belong to Royalty Industries.

Royalty Industries, Inc.

Snoopy Bank: 9in (23cm); vinyl ears; red felt costume; 1980s. **MARKS:** "Royalty Industries, Inc." on seal on foot. **SEE:** *Illustration 150. David Bausch Collection.*

Amscan, Inc.

Bendable Santa Claus: 11in (28cm); molded soft vinyl; the chimney is Santa's box, and he can squeeze back into it; 1978.

MARKS: "© 1978 Amscan, Inc.//Harrison N.Y." on chimney-box.

SEE: *Illustration 151.*

Delta Novelty Co.

Small Santa Claus Ornament: 4in (10cm); stuffed felt head; pipe cleaner body; net costume with fine gold wire holding material taut; sticker boots; 1970s.

This is an example of the many, many Christmas ornaments used to decorate trees, tables, packages and other holiday needs.

MARKS: "Delta Novelty Co. Japan" on gold tag.

SEE: *Illustration 151.*

Edwin M. Knowles China Company

American Santa Claus Checks His List: 13in (33cm); bisque head and hands; cloth body over armature; list of children's names in Santa's hand; 1989. This doll was designed by Faith Wick, and there is a facsimile of her autograph inside the tag.
MARKS: "1989 Knowles ©" on front of tag.
SEE: *Illustration 152. Shirley Karaba Collection.*

Dakin & Company (Vogue)

71-3010 Ginny Mr. & Mrs. Claus: 7in (18cm); vinyl; sleep eyes; dressed in traditional costumes of velvet; Mrs. Claus has a red and green print apron; 1986.

The doll is packaged in a winter scene with a pack of wrapped packages. The stands for each doll can be seen at the top. This was a limited edition for Shirley's Dollhouse.
MARKS: "A Real Vogue Doll" on gold heart wrist tag; "Ginny" on neck.
SEE: *Illustration 153.*

Effanbee Doll Corporation

Effanbee Christmas Collection (left to right):
Holly: 11in (28cm); vinyl; fully jointed; long black hair; red velvet dress trimmed in white; white scarf and hat trimmed with red felt band with holly; only 1500 manufactured and distributed to a select number of stores; 1983.
MARKS: "Effanbee" on back of head.
SEE: *Illustration 154.*
Effanbee Santa Claus: 11in (28cm); molded vinyl head with white beard and eyebrows; vinyl head and body with faux fur trim; black suede belt; tan suede toy pack; black boots; 1985.
MARKS: "Effanbee" on back of head.
SEE: *Illustration 154.*
Effanbee Mrs. Santa Claus: 11in (28cm); molded vinyl head and body; red and green print dress; white mob cap; white apron with "Mrs. Santa Claus" embroidered on it; white shoes and stocking; 1985.
MARKS: "Effanbee" on back of head.
SEE: *Illustration 154.*
Effanbee Snowman: 11in (28cm); molded white vinyl head; red nose; black eyes and dotted mouth; sleep eyes; stuffed flannel body; red striped scarf; molded black felt top hat; blue ear muffs.
MARKS: "Effanbee" on back of head.
SEE: *Illustration 154.*

The registered trademarks, the trademarks and copyrights appearing in italics//bold within this chapter belong to C.G.P.C. ©.

Country Gentlemen Pub. Co. David Grossman Designs

Norman Rockwell's "A Drum for Tommy:" 3½in (9cm); molded, painted bisque; Santa in the traditional red and white costume, carrying a brown bag of toys over his arm; made in Japan; 1979.

This is one of a series of Norman Rockwell Santa Clauses. They are Christmas tree ornaments.

MARKS: "C.G.P.C.//©1979" incised on bottom of stand; "A Dave Grossman Design" on seal on bottom of stand.

SEE: *Illustration 155.*

Nut Cracker Santa: Cast iron nut cracker which is cast to give the illusion of a sled; 5½in (14cm) nutcracker; 2½in (6cm); traditional red costume; green gloves; tan toy pack; 1989.

MARKS: "Canada" on base.

SEE: *Illustration 156. Phyllis S. Bechtold Collection.*

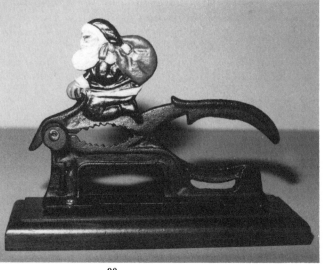

Steiff

Steiff Santa Claus Reproduction:
9in (23cm); felt doll and clothes; Germany; 1980s.
MARKS: "*Santa//Claus//Replica*" on button tag.
SEE: *Illustration 157. Linda Yonker Collection.*

Walt Disney Co.

Mickey Mouse Santa with Walking Stick: 8in (20cm); draped papier-mâché ; maroon Belsnickle-type costume; carries a pack of toys; green rope belt; black boots; 1989.

This Santa was featured in the new Disney stores which have opened all around the United States; 1990.

There is a matching *Minnie Mouse Mrs. Claus.*
MARKS: "*The Walt Disney Co.// 1989.*"
SEE: *Illustration 158.*

Battery Operated Santa in Car: 8in (20cm); vinyl Santa; plastic battery operated car; flashing lights; accompanied with electronic music; license plate says "1983."
SEE: *Illustration 159.*

The registered trademarks, the trademarks and copyrights appearing in italics//bold within this chapter belong to Sweet Dreams, Inc.

Sweet Dreams, Ltd.

Pepsi Stand-Up Santa Claus: 10½in (27cm); draped cloth over papier-mâché; plastic Pepsi-Cola cap hanging from belt; 1988.

The Stand-Up Santa Claus comes from the late 1940s advertisement shown on the tag Santa is holding.
MARKS: "'Clothtique Original'//by Sweet Dreams Ltd. 1989" on tag.
SEE: *Illustration 160.*

Annalee

Three Annalee Santas (from left to right):

1. **Santa and Toy Train:** 8in (20cm); cloth; velour pants; striped cotton shirt; bandana; felt boots; collector Santa with brass plaque. 1986.
MARKS: "Annalee '88//1986//Mobilite Dolls Inc.//Made only in Meredith, New Hampshire" on tag.
MARKS: "Time Out" on bronze plaque signed by Annalee.
SEE: *Illustration 161. Shirley Karaba Collection.*
2. **Santa Holding Brush and Wooden Toy Locomotive:** 18in (46cm); cloth; red flannel costume with plush trim; blue and white cobbler's apron; named "Workshop Santa."
MARKS: "Annalee '89//1967//1981//Mobilite Dolls, Inc.//Made only in Meredith, New Hampshire" on tag.
SEE: *Illustration 161. Shirley Karaba Collection.*
3. **Large Santa:** 18in (46cm); cloth; flannel suit and hat; plush trim; black felt boots; 1986.
MARKS: "Annalee ©//1967//Mobiltee Dolls, Inc.//Made only in Meredith, New Hampshire" on tag.
SEE: *Illustration 161. Shirley Karaba Collection.*

Cleveland Browns™ Santa Claus in Dirigible: 4in (10cm); vinyl; brown Santa Claus costume; 1990.
MARKS: "© Russ Berrie & Company, Inc.//NFL Official Licensed Product."
Santa Sun Bathing: 3in (8cm) tall by 5in (13cm) long; 1989.
MARKS: "Tis the Season// Browns™" on hat and stomach.

In the past few years the football and baseball leagues have given official approval to many Christmas products. Usually each item is available with the colors and names of each individual team in the league.
SEE: *Illustration 162. Wallace C. Judd Family Collection.*

Suncatcher: 5in (13cm); colored glass; 1980s.
SEE: *Illustration 163. Phyllis S. Bechtold Collection.*
Mr. and Mrs. Santa Claus on Park Bench: 5in (13cm) high; dolls are flexible vinyl; bench is rigid vinyl; 1970s.
MARKS: "Made in Hong Kong."
SEE: *Illustration 163.*

Annalee

Santa Mouse: 14in (36cm); felt gray mouse with pink ears; holly in hair; red felt coat and hat; quilted sack; 1971.
MARKS: "U.S.A.//Annalee® ©1971// Mobilite Doll//Inc. R//Meredith N.H."
SEE: *Illustration 164. Shirley Karaba Collection.*

Tin Star Santa: 3in (8cm); hand painted; 1986.
SEE: *Illustration 165.* (ornament on right) *Phyllis S. Bechtold Collection.*
Chinese Santa: 3in (8cm); plastic; jointed arms; molded painted facial features; black, slanted eyes; carrying yellow package; 1986.
MARKS: "China" base.
SEE: *Illustration 165.* (doll on left) *Phyllis S. Bechtold Collection.*

Santa Pull Toy: 8in (20cm) Santa dressed for work in his workshop; late 1980s.
SEE: *Illustration 166. Shirley Karaba Collection.*

95

The registered trademarks, the trademarks and copyrights appearing in italics//bold within this chapter belong to Walt Disney Enterprises.

Walt Disney Enterprises

Disney Micky and Minnie Santa and Mrs. Claus: 18in (46cm); 1988. **MARKS:** "Disneyland// Walt Disney World//© Disney" on tag. **SEE:** *Illustration 167.*

Civil-War (Patriotic) Santa Claus: 11in (28cm); modern fired clay base; blue coat with white stars; striped pants and hat; white fur-like trim; 1990.

This was made by an unknown local artist for sale in a gift shop in Berlin, Ohio. Its unique facial expression, attractive costume, and low price has made it a best-seller locally. **MARKS:** None. **SEE:** *Illustration 168.*

Christmas Reproductions Inc.

"These memories of Santa are authentic reproductions made from original antique chocolate molds. They depict the evolution of Santa Claus from the early St. Nicholas of 1820 to the Santa we know today. Although his garments changed by custom and his name changed from country to country, the generosity and spirit of old St. Nicholas survived through the ages to become the gift giving, Jolly Old Santa of our time."

Memories of Santa™ Collection: 4¾in (12cm); bisque; 1984.

The reproductions are:

Circa 1850. A very early St. Nicholas dressed in green robes.

Circa 1880. St. Nicholas carrying a bucket of ashes for bad boys and girls. He was known as "Ashenclos" in Germany.

Circa 1890. A fur-clad St. Nick, called "Pelze Nicol" by the children of northern Germany.*

Circa 1895. Kris Kringle Himself, a name coined by the Pennsylvania Dutch settlers.*

Circa 1905. Father Christmas, beloved by the children of Great Britain.

Circa 1915. An early Santa wearing blue trousers giving him a somewhat red, white and blue patriotic look to the people of the United States.

Circa 1920. Santa with the famous and popular "Teddy" Bear named after Theodore Roosevelt.*

Circa 1925. The most familiar Santa Claus, done up in his red costume with white trim.*

* Pictured

The information above is from a card which was packaged with the dolls.

SEE: *Illustration 169.*

Midwest Importers

Pantin-type Pull Toy:

This type of pull toy has been popular for hundreds of years. Children and adults are fascinated by the unique poses that are possible. Here are just two of the many Christmas Santas.

1. Doll on left: 5in (13cm); wood; legs jerk out when the string is pulled; 1983.

2. Doll on right: 10in (25cm); wood; unusual beige face; rings bell and limbs move when string is pulled; 1989.

MARKS: 1. None.

2. "Midwest Importers of Cannon Falls, Inc.//Made in Taiwan."

SEE: *Illustration 170.*

Authentic Models

Santa Claus Nesting Dolls: 2in (5cm), 2½in (6cm), 3in (8cm), 4in (10cm), 5in (13cm); all wood; hand painted; variations in types of Santas in different sets; largest Santa has a three-dimensional beard, mustache and eyebrows. 1991.

There have been many different Santa Claus nesting dolls over the years. This one is a current highly stylized version.

MARKS: None on dolls; "Made in China//For//Authentic Models//Handmade" on base.

SEE: *Illustration 171.*

Santa Fe Express: 3½in (9cm) by 14in (36cm); wood train with four cars; Santa is the engineer; engine; sleigh car; box car; caboose; painted in red, green, and white; 1988.
MARKS: "Made in Taiwan//Republic of China" on tag.
SEE: *Illustration 172.*

The registered trademarks, the trademarks and copyrights appearing in italics//bold within this chapter belong to Hallmark.

Hallmark

Hallmark Santa Claus Hot Dogger: 2½in (6cm); molded hard vinyl; 1987.
MARKS: "Hot Dogger// Handcrafted Ornament" on front of box; "Keepsake Ornament// 1987//Made in Macau" on back of box.
SEE: *Illustration 173.*

Walking Santa Claus Ringing Bell: 9½in (24cm); vinyl Santa Claus; plays three songs as it is walking, "I Wish You a Merry Christmas," "Santa Claus is Coming to Town" and "Jingle Bells;" 1987.
     Similar Santa Clauses played up to 12 songs.
MARKS: "Made in Taiwan" on box.
SEE: *Illustration 174.*

Christmas Corner

Patriotic Santa Claus: 9in (23cm); painted wood; large wooden mustache; carrying a red wooden star; 1990.

This doll was purchased at Strawbridge and Clothier Department Store in Philadelphia in 1990. They were featuring a "Red, White, and Blue Christmas" in all their stores that year.

MARKS: "Manufactured for//Christmas Corner//Sun Valley Ca. 91352 U.S.A.//Made in Philippines" on label.

SEE: *Illustration 175.*

Enesco

Modern Balloon Santa: Contemporary tin ornament by Enesco; late 1980s.

The tiny balloon Santa Claus is dwarfed by the large vintage print of Santa delivering presents in an old car.

SEE: *Illustration 176. David Bausch Collection.*

Chapter 6

Santa On Paper

Children have played with paper dolls since paper was invented. Santa Claus paper dolls go hand-in-hand with the larger and more expensive dolls and figures, and many collectors prefer to have the paper dolls because they are just as beautiful and easier to store.

The paper dolls in this chapter range from the 1870s until the present time. They include advertising paper dolls and other cut-outs, die-cut paper dolls, magazine paper dolls, paper dolls dressed in cotton batten wadding, and paper dolls to cut from wrapping paper. This is just a small sample of the lovely Santa paper dolls available to the collector today.

Santa on a Donkey: 7¼in (19cm); die-cut; "1873" pencilled on bottom of cut-out. **SEE:** *Illustration 177. Jayne Keller Collection.*

Cardboard Die-cut Santa: 8¾in (22cm); lightweight cardboard; long white costume with red boots, hat and bag; circa 1890s. **SEE:** *Illustration 178. Jayne Keller Collection.*

Die-cut Santa with Lantern: 12½in (32cm); embossed cardboard; circa 1895. **SEE:** *Illustration 179. Jayne Keller Collection.*

Advertising Santa to Hang on Christmas Tree (Santa on right): 10in (25cm); die-cut advertisement for Neuman's Ice Cream; circa 1920s.
MARKS: "Hang Me on Your Xmas Tree" on back of Santa.
SEE: *Illustration 180. Jayne Keller Collection.*
Santa Carrying Doll (Santa on left): 8½in (22cm); die-cut advertisement; 1919.
MARKS: "Christmas Savings Club//The Farmers' National Bank//Lititz, Pennsylvania."
SEE: *Illustration 180. Jayne Keller Collection.*

Paper Doll

Early Die-cut Paper Dolls: Santa and Little Girl inside Santa card; overall size 5¾in (17cm); clothing includes:

1. Upper Right: A1, blue coat trimmed with fur, hat, leggings set.
2. Lower Right: A2, red coat and hat trimmed with fur.
3. Upper Left: A3, yellow coat and hat trimmed with fur.
4. Upper Left: A4, white coat, hat and leggings trimmed with fur.

MARKS: "S & C. 380 A."
SEE: *Illustration 182. Mary Ann Hall Collection.*

The registered trademarks, the trademarks and copyrights appearing in italics//bold within this chapter belong to Willimantic Thread Co.

Willimantic Thread Co.

Advertising Postcard: 5¼in by 6¼in (13cm by 16cm); young boy with various costumes including an early version of Santa Claus carrying a tree; circa 1895.

Various types of cards were popular advertisements for many different companies in the late 1890s. Santa Claus and Christmas scenes were common. Many a collectible series of advertising paper toys were available for children who, like today's children, tried to get the entire series.

MARKS: "Presented//by// the Willimantic Thread Co." printed on the card.
SEE: *Illustration 181. Marlene Brenner Collection.*

Wadding Early Santa: 19in (48cm); die-cut scraps for arms, toys, feet and tree; cotton batting flat body; "December 1905" written on the back of the figure.
SEE: *Illustration 183. Mary Ann Hall Collection.*

Santa and Toy Cut-outs: Page from *McCall's Magazine*, December 1911: illustrated by John B. Gruelle for the story "Santa Claus and the Christmas Country." **SEE:** *Illustration 184. Jayne Keller Collection.*

Cut-out Santa, Christmas Tree, Sleigh, Toys: Page from unknown magazine; circa 1915. **SEE:** *Illustration 185. Jayne Keller Collection.*

German Walking Santa Claus: 6½in (17cm); die-cut with four revolving boots; Christmas tree ornament; circa 1920s. **MARKS:** "Made in Saxony" on back. **SEE:** *Illustration 186. Jayne Keller Collection.*

Advertising Santa: 6¼in (16cm); Bank Christmas Club advertisement from Kutztown National Bank, Kutztown, Pennsylvania; designed to be hung on the Christmas tree as an ornament; 1929. **MARKS:** "Kutztown National Bank" printed on front; "Hang Me on Your Christmas Tree" on back of card. **SEE:** *Illustration 187. Jayne Keller Collection.*

107

Kewpie Santa Claus: 11in (28cm); printed on light cardboard; red flocking on Santa hat; stand glued to back of doll.

This is an advertisement for the Royal Society, which made tinted stamped goods including pillows, dresser scarfs, bibs, fancy bags, and other novelties that could be embroidered.

MARKS: "I am the Kewpie Santa Claus" on the sign; "Kewpie//Copyrighted 1913// Patented March 14, 1914//Rose O'Neill (Signature)."

SEE: *Illustration 188.*

Pantin Jules Nisse and Helpers: 19½in by 14½in (50cm by 37cm); dressed in traditional Danish costumes; the helpers have wooden shoes; flag of Denmark in Jules Nisse's pocket; 1920s-1930s.

For more information about Jules Nisse and other Scandinavian gift-givers see page 146.

MARKS: None.

SEE: *Illustration 189.*

Foldout Paper Santa Claus: 66in (167cm).
1920s and 1930s.
  This unusually large Santa folds up into a
small package. When displayed full length,
Santa has a large "belly."
SEE: *Illustration 190.*

Advertisement for New England Mincemeat:
5½in (14cm); die-cut one-piece Santa Claus.
One of 16 dolls in the set of "The Fairy's
Children Who Ate the Fairy's Pie;" circa 1895.
MARKS: "New England//Mincemeat" printed
on back.
SEE: *Illustration 191. Jayne Keller Collection.*

Hidden Words Novelty: 6½in (17cm); beard moves and gives the advertising message from the First National Bank and Trust Co., Red Lion, Pennsylvania. The Santa on the left says, "Look under my beard"; 1921.
SEE: *Illustration 192. Jayne Keller Collection.*

Santa and His Sock: Page from *McCall's Magazine*, December 1923; illustrated by Berte and Elmer Hader.

Cut-outs help fill Santa's large sock.
SEE: *Illustration 193. Jayne Keller Collection.*

Santa's Stunt: Page from *Child Life*, December 1927. When put together correctly, Santa would go up and down the chimney and the little boy would appear at the window. **SEE:** *Illustration 194. Jayne Keller Collection.*

Winter Play with Santa Claus: 2½in to 5in (6cm to 13cm); die-cut; thick cardboard; each figure has a slotted green wooden stand; 1930s. **SEE:** *Illustration 195. Jayne Keller Collection.*

Animated Santa Toy Cut-outs:
Page from *Pictorial Review*,
December 1925.

Children were asked to follow
the directions for trimming the
tree and sorting out the gifts for
each paper toy.

Illustrated by K. Palleson.
SEE: *Illustration 196. Jayne
Keller Collection.*

*The registered trademarks, the
trademarks and copyrights
appearing in italics//bold within
this chapter belong to Grace
Drayton.*

Dolly Dingle's Christmas:
Drawn by Grace Drayton; toys
and clothes for Dolly Dingle;
Pictorial Review, December
1929.
SEE: *Illustration 197.*

Die-cut Santas with Movable Legs: 5¾in (15cm), 11in (28cm), 18½in (48cm); 1930s. **MARKS:** "Made in U.S.A." on back. **SEE:** *Illustration 198. Jayne Keller Collection.*

Two-sided, Mirror Image Early Santa (Santa on right): 7in (18cm); ornament to hang on tree; early 1900s.
SEE: *Illustration 199. Jayne Keller Collection.*
Kiddie Cut-out Santa Claus (Santa on left): 3in by 5in (8cm by 13cm); one of a set of 24 cut-outs used as advertisements for Dawdy's Bread; circa 1920s-1930s.
MARKS: "Dawdy's Bread" on back of card.
SEE: *Illustration 199. Jayne Keller Collection.*

PULL

PULL

Slide-A-Card Santa: When the card at the bottom is pulled, Santa comes down through the chimney into the fireplace; 1930s.

The pull cards says "Dear Children, write me a letter telling what kind of Endicott Johnson shoes you want for Christmas. Be sure to tell me your correct size. Send your letter to me at the address on the back of this card, and they will see that I get it. You will like these shoes. They are dandy-looking, comfortable, and long wearing. Merry Christmas to all. Santa Claus."
SEE: *Illustration 200. Jayne Keller Collection.*

Card, Calendar, Santa Claus: 6in (15cm); paper ornament Santa Claus which could be detached from card and calendar; 1960. (1962 Calendar.)
MARKS: "Copyright 1960 Christmas Club, a Corporation, New York N.Y. Litho in U.S.A." on bottom of card.
SEE: *Illustration 201. Jayne Keller Collection.*

Paper Santa Claus Bank: 6in
(15cm) long; double-sided paper
sleigh that folds to form a bank;
promotion from First National Bank
of Allentown, Pennsylvania; 1964.
MARKS: "Season's Greetings//
First//National Bank//of Allentown."
SEE: *Illustration 202. Jayne Keller*
Collection.

The registered trade-
marks, the trademarks
and copyrights appearing
in italics//bold within this
chapter belong to Gordon
Fraser Ref W.R. 865.

Wrapping Paper Santa
and Mrs. Claus with
Costumes: 19in by 13½in
(48cm by 34cm); late
1980s.
MARKS: "A Gordon
Fraser Wrapper Ref W.R.
865 Printed in England"
at bottom of sheet.
SEE: *Illustration 203.*

Season's Greetings from your
Coca-Cola Bottler: Package
decorations; Santa Claus, angel and
Christmas Girl paper dolls to cut out
and put on top of your packages.

The messages on the cut-out
says, "SANTA CLAUS — who
knows what he looks like? Children
do, and have, since 1931 when
American artist Haddon Sundblom
first created 'Santa' as a kindly,
white-bearded old gentleman who
held in his hand a frosty bottle of
Coca-Cola."
SEE: *Illustration 204.*

Chapter 7

Contemporary Doll Artist's Santa Clauses

Many artists are creating Santa Claus dolls and figures that are selling well. The ones shown in this chapter are from contemporary artists who are either creating limited editions or one-of-a-kind Santas in many price ranges.

Some of these dolls recreate the old Santas of the past. Others are fantasy dolls designed by the artist. Some, like Ben Franklin, show a new look at historical figures.

There are hundreds of new dolls being sold today. The dolls shown here were chosen because they are from different parts of the United States, and one is from Germany. The prices are the original prices when sold to the first customer.

Stanley Wanlass

One-of-a-Kind Jalopy with Santa: 16in (41cm) high; 24in (61cm) long; sculptor, Stanley Wanlass; the banner lists girls and boys including the owner's and the sculptor's friends.
SEE: *Illustration 205. David Bausch Collection.*

116

Peter Wolf — Germany

Father Christmas: 17in (43cm); synthetic composition; carries the traditional toys and switches, a Christmas tree and wreath; dressed in green velvet, trimmed in fur.

Peter Wolf uses no molds and is not interested in the reproduction of his dolls in limited editions. Each doll is individually sculpted and crafted, creating a new and unique rendition each time.

The doll has a traditional construction, like the old church figures with a padded wire armature. The head, hands and legs are modeled, fired and painted. The compound from which the doll is made is as hard as china and just as permanent.
SEE: *Illustration 206. Phyllis S. Bechtold Collection.*

Marilyn McElroy — California

Santa: Made by Marilyn McElroy who works in the design department of Mattel.
SEE: *Illustration 207. Linda Yonker Collection.*

Deborah Kubilus — Massachusetts

Wax Musical Automotion: 17in (43cm); wax face and hands; dressed in red velvet robes; small feather tree; pack of wonderful toys including a tiny China-head doll; made by doll artist Deborah Kubilus; 1986.
MARKS: "Deborah Kubilus//11/24/86."
SEE: *Illustration 208. Phyllis S. Bechtold Collection.*

G. Alexander

Birdhouse Gourd: 11in (28cm); natural gourd; hand painted; artist is G. Alexander; 1990s.
SEE: *Illustration 209. John Bechtold Collection.*

118

Laura Turner — Maryland

Santa Claus: 20in (51cm); molded mask face; hat and body out of an old quilt; Frizzleburg, Maryland.
SEE: *Illustration 210. Linda Yonker Collection.*

Bessie Kuehny — Ohio

Santa and Mrs. Claus: 5½in (14cm); cloth; embroidered features; yarn hair; red felt Santa costume and black felt boots; red and white calico dress trimmed in eyelet; organdy apron; pantaloons; black felt shoes for Mrs. Claus.
MARKS: "Bessie Kuehny" on tag of Santa Claus.
"Bess Kuehny Original" on paper pinned to dress of Mrs. Claus.
SEE: *Illustration 211. Barbara Comienski Collection. Photograph by Jim Comienski.*

Beverly Cope — Idaho

Group of Santa Claus Dolls by Beverly Cope: Includes Santa Claus, Nast Santa Claus, Father Christmas, St. Nick, and two antique reproductions.
SEE: *Illustration 212. Beverly Cope Collection.*

The registered trademarks, the trademarks and copyrights appearing in italics//bold within this chapter belong to Kerin's Collectibles.

Kerin Houseburg — Ohio

Carved Wooden Santa Claus: 16½in (42cm); carved wooden face with beard, lower arms and legs; cloth body; painted features; maroon cotton trousers, blue sweater under robes, forest green loden cloth robe trimmed in lambswool; carries walking stick; fur and burlap toy bag on back; wood and cloth toys dangle from belt; 1990.
MARKS: "Kerin's Collectibles// Kerin Houseburg" on paper tag.
SEE: *Illustration 213. Barbara Comienski Collection. Photograph by Jim Comienski.*

R. John Wright — New York

St. Nicholas: 17in (43cm); felt; red velvet, monk-type hooded robes with long sleeves; painted face; mohair wig and beard; "carpet-type" pack; handmade wooden cross held together with leather thongs; triple-seamed ear; one of R. John Wright's early dolls.
MARKS: "#151 of Edition of 250;" on hang tag; "NIADA Certified Doll" sewn on tag in back of doll; "Wright" on left foot.
SEE: *Illustration 214. Marianne Gardner Collection.*
Shepherdess: 17in (43cm); dark felt; cotton underwear, striped cotton skirt, white ascot, orange felt jerkin, embroidered slippers, orange felt hat; mohair wig; triple-seamed ear; one of R. John Wright's early dolls.
MARKS: "NIADA Certified Doll" sewn on tag in back; "WRIGHT" written on left foot.
SEE: *Illustration 214. Marianne Gardner Collection.*
Seth, Farmer with Pitchfork: 17in (43cm); felt; red leather laced boots; chino pants, plaid shirt, leather and elastic suspenders; black mixed with gray mohair wig and beard; triple-seamed ear; one of R. John Wright's early dolls.
MARKS: "NIADA Certified Doll" sewn on tag in back; "WRIGHT" written on left foot.
SEE: *Illustration 214. Marianne Gardner Collection.*

Patricia L. Wilson —Michigan

Nature Santa Claus: 21in (53cm); porcelain head and hands; armature for movement; stuffed body; wooden base; beard and wig are made from Michigan Lincoln wool, cleaned and combed by the artist; the robe is made of velvet, brocade and wool; 1992.

This Father Christmas carries a bird in a cage, animals and fruits of nature. These are symbols of good luck, health and happiness throughout the year.

MARKS: Signed and numbered on the base by the artist. There are 200 in the edition. Included is a Certificate of Authenticity.

SEE: *Illustration 215. Patricia L. Wilson Collection.*

Kay Laughlin — Ohio

Folk Art Replica of Antique Toy: 20in (51cm); flat piece of wood for chimney. Santa 5in (13cm); painted wood. Santa seesaws down pegs on a midnight blue, snow-flaked backdrop into a wooden chimney.

MARKS: "Kay" on bottom of chimney.

SEE: *Illustration 216. Barbara Comienski Collection. Photograph by Jim Comienski.*

Judy Tasch — Texas

Father Christmas: 18in (46cm); leather face, wool clothes trimmed in real fur; Austin, Texas. **SEE:** *Illustration 217. Linda Yonker Collection.*

The registered trademarks, the trademarks and copyrights appearing in italics//bold within this chapter belong to Bit of Christmas.

Bit of Christmas — New Jersey

Father Franklin: 18in (46cm); modern composition head; spongy-type body, and arms and legs which have a poseable armature inside body; painted face with gold Benjamin Franklin-type glasses; maroon velvet coat, lace jabot, ornate vest of tapestry material, black pants; Christmas season 1990.

Strawbridge and Clothier featured a patriotic Christmas theme in all their stores in 1990. The Ben Franklin dolls were only sold at their main store in downtown Philadelphia. The edition is limited to 150 dolls. *Father Franklin* is carrying a 7in (18cm) Christmas tree and several wrapped packages. He is also weighted down with articles that celebrate his many accomplishments in life.

Father Franklin has a kite with a key on the string, a small blackboard with "Poor Richard's Almanac 1732" written on it, a piece of parchment with a hand written section of the Declaration of Independence, a letter to the Postmaster General of Philadelphia, and even a peacock feather.
MARKS: "Bit of Christmas//Stockton-Lambertville, New Jersey" on tag.
SEE: *Illustration 218.*

Stone Soup Designs, Inc., Shelie and Richard McCall — California

Stone Soup Black Father Christmas: 50in (127cm); face hand-sculpted in clay (Each face is done individually.); the cape is made of old mohair; the robe is cut velvet (Vintage fabrics are used for the costumes.); accessories include a replica ship of the type used by Christopher Columbus in 1492, a teddy bear, candle, small Christmas tree, pine cones, holly berries, and pine needles.

The ship celebrates the 500th Anniversary of the Discovery of America.
SEE: *Illustration 219. Shelie and Richard McCall Collection.*

Chapter 8

Santa Claus and Other Bearers of Gifts from Around the World

The Santa Claus and other gift-bearers' legends originate in the story of the Magi coming from afar and bringing gifts to the Christ Child. Today the international legends of Santa Claus reflect the culture and environment of the people of each country, province, town, village, and family, who have added their own customs to the Christmas gift-giving tradition.

Through the years, dolls and figures have helped preserve these traditions and legends, and this chapter shows some of them. The international gift-bearers include ordinary men and women, animals, saints, angels, and jolly elves. Children in each country understand their own gift-bearers, but most of them also recognize and smile when they see a Santa Claus in the familiar red suit.

Many Christmas traditions are changing around the world. Santa Claus waterskis into Australia, runs rapids in Amazonian jungles, and crosses a South Seas lagoon in a catamaran. Santas of all races and nationalities sit in department stores in many countries of the world greeting children. Santa has found his way to Hong Kong and other Asiatic countries where he is known as "Christmas Old Man." He also continues to come down American chimneys.

Children, and most adults, seem to understand that Santa Claus, like Mickey Mouse and Coca Cola, is a symbol of happiness and "the good life." The Italian Santa Claus in *Illustration 221* seems to sum up the world-wide philosophy very well. The nesting doll is a Santa Claus on the outside, a Christmas tree in the center, and finally a tiny angel bearing the greatest gift of all. On her dress is painted a one word message to people everywhere — "Pax."

The Coming of the Magi to the Manger: 18in by 20½in (46cm by 52cm); wood manger; figures are from 7½in (19cm) to 12in (31cm); music box plays "Silent Night."

This is the traditional crèche scene often found in homes around the world during the Christmas holidays. Many people believe that Santa Claus and other gift-givers originated in the story of the Magi.

Like many other crèches, this one was handed down from Wally Judd's grandmother to his family.

MARKS: "Made in Italy."

SEE: *Illustration 220. Wallace C. Judd Family Collection.*

Italy

Italian Nesting Santa Claus: 8½in (22cm); all-painted wood construction; 1977.

MARKS: "Pax" on the front of the angel.

SEE: *Illustration 221.*

The registered trademarks, the trademarks and copyrights appearing in italics//bold within this chapter belong to M.E. Duncan.

Duncan, M.E. Company (Duncan Royale)

In the early part of the 1980s, Duncan Royale presented a limited edition of 24 figurines entitled "The Complete History of Santa." In 1987 the company published a hardback book with the same title so it could expand the legends of the figurines. Both the beautiful book and the figurines are still available today, but a few of the figurines have been "retired," and new ones have been added.

The ceramic figurines have been made in both 6in (15cm) and 12in (31cm) sizes. Duncan Royale also makes 2¼in (6cm) pewter miniatures. The gift-bearers in the photographs are 6in (15cm).

From left to right:

Medieval St. Nicholas: Shown here as a gift bearer wandering the world before legends gave him the ability to fly.

Wassail: The figure of a caroler is holding the wassail bowl filled with spiced ale with toasted apples floating in it. This is an English custom during the Yule season.

Pioneer: The American image of Santa Claus changed as the country grew and brought in a tide of immigrants. His size and clothes resembled the customs and attire of the new citizens. He is pictured here as a frontier man moving westward. He is carrying a Christmas tree decorated with American flags to the children in their new prairie homes.

Bavarian (Christkindt): A less formal St. Nicholas helps the young Christkindt distribute gifts to Bavarian children.

MARKS: Gold plaque on base of sculpture.

SEE: *Illustration 222.*

Black Peter: In the early Dutch legends Black Peter was a form of the Devil. Later Christmas legends changed him into a companion of St. Nicholas and other gift givers. It was often his duty to determine who the bad children were and "reward" them with sticks or coal. This figure carries brass switches in a pack on his back. There are many names for Black Peter in other countries. A few of these companions deliver gifts as well as punishments.

Civil War Santa: During the Civil War Thomas Nast pictured Santa in a red, white, and blue costume which looked like a version of the American flag.

Victorian Santa Claus: This is a very dignified English Father Christmas.

Dedt Moroz: Father Ice of Russia rewards the good and punishes the bad children.

MARKS: Gold plaque on base of sculpture.

SEE: *Illustration 223.* (Also see Pages 130 and 131 for more illustrations.)

Czechoslovakia

Grup vom Krampus: Postcard sent in Germany; 1920s.

Marionette: 7in (18cm) bisque head, arms and legs; wood body; excellent sculpting and painting on face; hands wired to black cape so that the marionette could appear to fly; red and gold *Grup Von Krampus* costume; 1920s.

MARKS: "Made in Czechoslovakia" on a paper sticker on the bottom of the left foot.

SEE: *Illustration 225.* Opposite page.

The people of middle Europe have various names for the companion who accompanies St. Nicholas on his rounds. They include Hans Muff, Knecht Rupprecht, Butz, Hans Tripp, Grup vom Krampus, Klaubauf, Bartel, Perchtha, Buzebergt, Budelfrau, Buttenmandin, Pelznickel, the Berchtenrunner Mob, and Habersack. Some bring presents of coal or switches. Others take the presents away. There are many variations in the spellings of their names.

Krampus has a long tail, a red, snake-like tongue and he carries a basket of switches on his back.

Australia

Australian Santa Claus in Bathing Suit: 3½in (9cm); painted bisque; tan Australian hat; red, green and yellow bathing suit; 1989.

This set of Christmas decorations is the first in a series designed by one of Australia's most popular illustrators, award-winning Roland Harvey.

A trip to the beach is very popular in Australia on Christmas day. For many years, Santa Claus has been pictured arriving by boat, surfboard or water skis.

MARKS: "Roland//© 1989// Harvey" on a tag on the bottom of the foot.

SEE: *Illustration 224.*

Duncan, M.E. Company (Duncan Royale)

Brochure Showing All 24 of The History of Santa Figures:

From left to right:
Row 1. **Odin, Lord of Misrule, Mongolian/Asian, The Magi.**
Row 2. **Alsace Angel, Frau Holda, Sir Christmas, The Pixie.**
Row 3. **Medieval, Russia, Wassail, Kris Kringle.**
SEE: *Illustration 226. Used by Permission of Max E. Duncan.*

From left to right:
Row 1. **St. Lucia, Befana, Babouska of Russia; Bavarian.**
Row 2. **St. Nicholas, Dedt Moroz, Black Peter, Victorian**
Row 3. **Soda Pop, Pioneer, Civil War, Nast.**
SEE: *Illustration 227. Used by Permission of Max. E. Duncan.*

China

Chinese Balloon Santa Claus: 24in (61cm); vinyl balloon-type body; 1983.

In China Santa Claus and Mickey Mouse have become very familiar to children. Mickey and Santa balloon dolls are now a welcome sight for children all year around in a toy store in the southern inland city of Kweilin. The children in and around the store were very excited when one of the Santas hanging from the ceiling was sold to Polly Judd. They smiled and shouted in English, "Christmas Old Man bring gifts." As Mrs. Judd walked away with her Santa Claus, the children turned back to the television set in the town square.
MARKS: None.
SEE: *Illustration 228.*

Czechoslovakia

Santa from Czechoslovakia: 10in (25cm); papier-mâché face and body; rabbit fur beard; red coat, blue pants; carrying two woven baskets; 1930s.
MARKS: "1930" on the bottom of the skis.
SEE: *Illustration 229. David Bausch Collection.*

Italy

La Befana: 12in (31cm); clay head; cloth body; wearing the traditional fur-lined cloak, red scarf, and carrying a broom, switches, a lantern to light her way, and a bag full of toys for boys and girls. In Italy she leaves gifts for good children and switches for bad on the Eve of Epiphany, January 5.

A legend says that an old woman was sweeping her house when three richly dressed gentlemen asked her the way to find the new-born baby in Bethlehem. She did not want to leave her house and so refused to go. She finished her sweeping and followed them alone. She lost her way and for thousands of years she has roamed the earth in all kinds of weather looking for the Baby and leaving gifts for children.

The doll was made by Pam Judd and is one-of-a-kind.

MARKS: None.

SEE: *Illustration 230.*

The registered trademarks, the trademarks and copyrights appearing in italics//bold within this chapter belong to The Toy Works.

Saint Nicholas

Sinterklass (St. Nicholas): 14½in (37cm); all-cloth; pattern printed on material; cut out and sewn; special design by Toy Works, Inc.; 1975.

St. Nicholas was the Archbishop of Myra in Asia Minor during the 4th century. He

was known for his good deeds and saintly ways. He was especially known for the story of providing a dowry for poor girls who otherwise could not get married. He also did many good deeds for boys and is considered one of their patron saints.

His fame spread into many countries including those in Europe which still consider him the primary gift-bearer of the Christmas season. St. Nicholas arrives on his special day, which is December 7, and along with Zwart Piet (Black Peter), who carries switches for bad children, arrives in special ceremonies in each country. In some countries he is honored along with different gift-bearers. These countries include Poland (Svatej Nikulas), Netherlands (Sinterklass), Czechoslovakia (Svaty Nikalas), Italy (San Nicola), Bavaria (Nikolo-Weibl), and Syria (St. Nikolas Thaumaturgis).

The long-bearded bishop wears a white robe, crimson cassock, and tall miter (official headdress). He wears white gloves on his hands and carries a gold-colored crozier shaped like a shepherd's crook. Black Peter dresses like a medieval page.

MARKS: "The Toy Works, Inc. 1975//Middle Falls, N.Y. 12848" stamped on bottom of doll.

SEE: *Illustration 231.*

The registered trademarks, the trademarks and copyrights appearing in italics//bold within this chapter belong to Sears Roebuck & Co.

Sears Roebuck & Co.

Bearers of Gifts:
    December is a month of festivity and gift giving around the world. Each country has its own traditions and legends, and the small international dolls and figures made each year for decorations often have these legends printed on tags and brochures attached to them. The legends are as much fun to collect as the dolls themselves. Each tag also has the Christmas greeting of the country in the language spoken in that country.
    Sears Roebuck & Co.: Each doll from Sears is approximately 4in (10cm); all-wood; brightly painted faces and costumes; has a gold circular tag which explains the Christmas legend represented by the doll.
Greece: Man carrying a cross and a net with fish caught in it. The legend says, "on 'Greek Cross Day' in January, the priest tosses a cross into the sea. Young men dive to recover it, and the successful one is blessed bringing good fortune." 1981.
German Christangel: Carries Christmas tree. The story says, "In German homes, a young girl dresses as an angel with golden wings and crown and carries a tiny Christmas tree." 1980.
Christmas Greeting: "Weihnachten."
American Traditional: Williamsburg traditional festivities include various ceremonies, simple decorations for the home and lighting of the community tree. 1980.
Christmas Greeting: "Merry Christmas."
MARKS: "Sears Roebuck and Co.//(date)//Taiwan R.O.C." on a seal on the dolls from 1980-1981.
SEE: *Illustration 232.*

Austria: "In Austria the 'Stollen' is a special Christmas gift cake...famous also throughout Germany." 1981.
Christmas Greeting: "Frohliche Weihnachten."
China: "In China children hang up their stockings and hope that Santa Claus (Oun Che Lao Ren-Christmas Old Man) will fill them with toys, dolls, and candy." No date on doll.
Spain: "In Spain children fill their shoes with carrots or hay for the Three Kings' hungry camels to eat on their way to Bethlehem."
Christmas Greeting: "Felices Pascuas." No date on doll.
Denmark: "In Denmark even the birds are included in the Christmas festivities. Early Christmas morning each household sets out a gift of seeds and wheat stalks for the birds. 1982.
Christmas Greeting: "Glaedelig Jul."
MARKS: "Sears Roebuck and Co.//(1982)//Handcrafted in Taiwan" on a seal on the dolls.
SEE: *Illustration 233.*

Germany

Knecht Reprecht (doll on left): 16in (41cm); sculpted composition head; cloth body over armature; dressed in faux lambskin robe with hood; brown velvet ribbon and sack with brown Santa suit underneath; 1991.

A legend card that comes with doll says, "Knecht Ruprecht is a very old German personage. He dates back before Christianity. He is sometimes the punishing companion with Saint Nicholas or the Christkind, and in other times he is the gift bringer. Original ethnic representations researched and made by June & Bob Tressler."
MARKS: A legend card comes with doll.
SEE: *Illustration 234.*

Christkind (doll in middle): 13in (33cm); sculpted composition head; cloth body over armature; white angel costume; white and silver ribbon trim; gold wings; gold crown with stars; carries Christmas tree and basket of fruit; 1991.

A legend card that comes with doll says, "Christkind arrives at homes by climbing down from heaven on a golden cord. She is a mere messenger, for the gifts she brings are direct from the Christ child. She is usually accompanied by a punishing companion. Original ethnic representations researched and made by June & Bob Tressler."
MARKS: A legend card comes with the doll.
SEE: *Illustration 234.*

Christmann (doll on right): 18in (46cm); sculpted composition head; cloth body over armature; long white coat with gold buckle; white top hat with red ribbon; white cotton undersuit; white top hat with red ribbon; carries fruit and nuts in pockets; boy doll in left pocket; 1991.

A legend card that comes with doll says, "Christmann comes in an area called Ruppin, riding a great white horse. He has large pockets on his coat filled with candies, fruits, nuts and small toys. He is at times accompanied by dark figures dressed in raggy women's clothing. The procession usually goes from house to house. Original ethnic representations researched and made by June & Bob Tressler."
MARKS: A legend card comes with the doll.
SEE: *Illustration 234.*

Austria

Pull-String Santa Claus: 7in (18cm); all-wood; painted.

In Austria Santa Claus figures are also called Budelfrau, Schmalzli.

UNUSUAL IDENTIFYING FEATURE: The pink color, instead of red, on modern Austrian Santa Clauses is different from that used in other countries making Santa Claus and Christmas ornaments.

MARKS: "Made in Austria" stamped on back.

SEE: *Illustration 235.*

Caribbean Islands

Straw Santa: 11in (28cm); from one of the Caribbean Islands; sponge body; raffia beard; straw face and hands; 1970s-1980s.

SEE: *Illustration 236. Phyllis S. Bechtold Collection.*

Taiwan

St. Nicholas: 7in (18cm); doll made of bamboo with carved details; the beard and eyebrows are shaved bamboo; 1967.

MARKS: None.

SEE: *Illustration 237. Laura May Brown Collection.*

England

Mummers (doll on left): 16in (41cm); sculpted composition head; cloth body over armature; dark green wool coat trimmed with white; wreath on head; carries a basket of apples and nuts; 1991.

A legend card that comes with doll says, "Mummers were a group of street actors who for hundreds of years traveled about performing traditional plays. One of the characters in their Christmas play was Old Father Christmas. Since the late 19th century when Father Christmas became a gift bringer, the Mummers' portrait of this character was the greatest influence in his appearance in the 20th century. Original ethnic representations researched and made by June & Bob Tressler."

This doll also resembles the original illustrations of The Ghost of Christmas Present in Charles Dickens' *Christmas Carol*.

MARKS: A legend card comes with the doll.
SEE: *Illustration 238.*

Lithuania

Zimiemnik (doll on right): 16in (41cm); sculpted composition head; cloth body over armature; long loden green coat with fur trim; gold rope belt with bells on end; carries two sticks; 1991.

The legend card that comes with the doll says, "Zimiemnik was once the ancestral god of the family. He at one time made his visits during the Winter Solstice period. After the country became Christian his visits came on New Year's Day. He would welcome in the luck of the New Year by throwing corn or ashes on the family fire, causing sparks to fly. The number of sparks foretold the size of the farmer's herd for the coming year. He would sometimes throw his corn at members of the household to bring them luck. The nuts and apples the children received were not only treats but were ways of foretelling each child's future. Original ethnic representations researched and made by June & Bob Tressler."

MARKS: A legend card comes with the doll.
SEE: *Illustration 238.*

The registered trademarks, the trademarks and copyrights appearing in italics//bold within this chapter belong to the House of Nisbet.

England

Peggy Nisbet Dolls: 8in (20cm), vinyl-plastic compound; early 1980s. From left to right: **Santa Claus in America; Kris Kringle; Hote Iosha** (Japanese Santa); **St. Nicholas in Europe.** SEE: *Illustration 239. Linda Yonker Collection.*

England

Father Christmas in Britain: 8in (20cm); vinyl-plastic compound; dressed in long red flannel robe, trimmed with mock fur; black belt with large gold buckle; carries brown burlap bag; 1983-1984.

MARKS: None on doll; "A Peggy Nisbet Model//8334//Father Christmas in Britain//Made in England" on wrist tag. SEE: *Illustration 240.*

140

Switzerland

Musical Santa Claus: 8in (20cm); knit cloth body; painted face; red felt coat with Swiss flowered trim; green felt hat with bell used as tassel; green felt shoes; 1970s. In some areas of Switzerland, he is called Samichlaus. When a string is pulled from the back of the doll, a music box plays "Im Waid Und Auf Der Heide." The string gradually retreats into the body as the song ends.

MARKS: "Swiss Musical Movement" on a seal on the back.

SEE: *Illustration 241,* below.

Poland

Polish Santa Claus: 7½in (19cm); all-wood; dressed in traditional Santa Claus costume; 1950s-1960s.

MARKS: "Made in Poland" sticker on bottom of right shoe.

SEE: *Illustration 242,* above.

France

In Provence in the south of France, Christmas is celebrated with gaiety. A large log is put in the fireplace and kept burning until New Year's Day.

Children find rocks, branches and moss to build the settings for the "Cribs" which are featured in houses and churches throughout the region. Terra cotta figures, known as "Santons" (little Saints) are made in Provence. Santons join the Wise Men bearing gifts to the Christ Child. Not only are the traditional manger figures used, but people of the towns and villages are also represented in the scenes. Such figures as farmers, policemen, butchers, bakers, artists, and many others are collected over the years.

Some families make their own figures, others buy them from specific Santon makers each year, and many families collect representatives from different sources. The "Crib" scenes usually contain hills, valleys and other features of Provence. Roads are also made in the scenes so that the Santons can journey easily to see the Christ Child.

These Santons range in size from about 1in (3cm) to life-size figures. Some are very primitive; others are beautiful art objects. Santons have been sold in other countries of the world for many years. The dolls in *Illustration 243* are representative of the thousands made annually and others carefully preserved from the past. One of the most beautiful sets of Santons can be found in the Musée National of Monaco.

Farmer and Wife Santons: 10in (25cm); terra cotta; excellent sculpting; dressed in costumes of Provence; lady dressed in blue flowered dress and white scarf with lace trim; man dressed in traditional blue pants, striped shirt, and red tie at waist; both are carrying grain as gifts; early 1980s.

MARKS: "S. Jouglas" carved on base of each doll; "Made in France//imported by//Blyth Imports" on a seal on the bottom of the base.

SEE: *Illustration 243*.

France

Pére Noël: 30in (76cm); sculpted, painted composition face; cloth body; arms and legs cloth over armature; long dark red velvet robe trimmed in white fur, long red dress under robe; carrying musical instrument, toys and doll; toys and fruit in basket; 1991.

A legend card that comes with doll says, "French Pére Noël who brought gifts to children of Noblemen in the Victorian Era. Original ethnic representations research and made by June & Bob Tressler." **MARKS:** A legend card comes with the doll. **SEE:** *Illustration 244. Bob and June Tressler Collection.*

Mexico

The Mexican people love the Christmas season. They decorate with colorful flowers, such as the poinsettia which blooms in December, balloons, piñatas, and candles to light the way for the Christ Child. The nine days of the Christmas "Posada" begin on December 16, and the Christmas story is reenacted daily. On Christmas Eve the Christ Child is placed in the crèche.

Santa Claus has not been the traditional "gift-giver" in Mexico, but in the last half of the 20th century he has become part of the celebrations. Santa has joined the processions along with the Three Kings and the Holy Family.

Santa dolls, figures, ornaments, and piñatas can be found in shops, advertisements and homes. Tourists can purchase Mexican Santas any time of the year when they visit Mexico.

Traditional Greeting: "Feliz Navidad."

Mexico

Piñata Santa Claus: 25in (64cm); papier-mâché body; red, white and blue paper Santa costume; 1981.

A piñata is used as a treat for Mexican children all year at parties or holiday celebrations. One child is blindfolded and tries to hit and break open the piñata with a stick. The small toys and candies stored in the figure tumble out, and all the children scramble for their share (See *Illustration 246.*)
MARKS: None.
SEE: *Illustration 245.*

Mexico

Santa Claus with Umbrella (doll on left): 6in (15cm); draped paper and cotton batting; small bell in left hand; 1991.
Basket Scene of Children Breaking Piñata: 5½in (14cm); woven wooden basket; grass and children of Sculpy-type material which has been painted and lacquered.
MARKS: None.
SEE: *Illustration 246.*

The registered trademarks, the trademarks and copyrights appearing in italics//bold within this chapter belong to Charlotte Weibull.

Sweden

Charlotte Weibull of Akarp, Sweden has long been one of the leading authorities on the costumes and traditions of her country. Her dolls are sought by collectors around the world and her costumes are used for dances, plays and other traditional Swedish get-togethers. Weibull's dolls usually come with information that explains the costume and the legends. Her Christmas dolls offer unusual insight into Christmases of the past, as celebrated in Sweden.

Goanisse (doll on left): 7in (18cm); cloth over armature; painted stockinette head; yarn hair; gray wool suit, red hat, scarf, mittens, and stockings; wooden shoes; late 1970s.

The little pamphlet is in the box with the *Goanisse* says, "In the days when my grandmother was a girl, Father Christmas was unknown in Osterlen. At that time there was someone else called 'Goanisse.' He was a sort of farmhand and was described as a little man dressed in rough gray clothes and wearing a pointed red cap. Families seemed to have their own 'Goanisse' who did the rounds during the silent hours of the night, watching over man and beast."

MARKS: "Charlotte Weibull" on armband. **SEE:** *Illustration 247.*

Tomtes (small doll in middle): 3½in (9cm); mask face; wound yarn body; red outer garment, gray undergarment; late 1970s.

The pamphlet with the doll explains, "The Tomtes are kind, generous, and friendly little people dressed in gray with knitted red caps and scarves. They are ideal for decorating the Christmas table, together with fur cones, branches and moss which can be gathered in the woods."

MARKS: None. **SEE:** *Illustration 247.*

Luciafirandet (St. Lucia) (doll on right): 5½in (14cm); painted, mask face; cloth over wood body; dressed in a white long dress with a red sash; lingon or whortleberry leaf crown into which white lighted candles are inserted; late 1970s.

The Feast of Lights is celebrated on the 13th of December, the feast day of St. Lucia. Tradition says that a young girl (some say the youngest daughter and others say the oldest) announces the day by serving everyone in the family breakfast in bed. This honors the 4th century Sicilian saint who was killed rather than marry a pagan.

MARKS: None. **SEE:** *Illustration 247.*

According to Charlotte Weibull, "Today in Sweden, the gift-giver is usually Father Christmas who generally has a long red coat set off with a long white beard. His ancestors came from England and Germany, and in contrast to the small gray Jultomtes, he is tall and well-built."

Scandinavia

The Scandinavian countries of Norway, Sweden, Denmark, and Finland are all located in northern Europe. They have many common bonds, including their Christmas legends. Their Christmas spirits are all small gnome or elf-like creatures. Jultomaten (Jultomte) is from Sweden, Julenisse is from Norway (and possibly Denmark), and Nisse is from Denmark. They are mischievous beings who demand food at Christmas time, or they will play serious tricks on the household. They may also help around the farms or houses. Many Scandinavians also believe they bring the gifts at Christmas. Joulupukki from Finland has the costume of a goat with horns mounted on his head. A common Christmas greeting in Scandinavia is "God Jul."

God Jul Doll: 11in (28cm); all-wood; painted body; red knit hat; carries burlap bag; 1979.

MARKS: "Made in Sweden" on bottom of shoe.

SEE: *Illustration 248.*

Italy

Babbo Natale: 9½in (24cm); entirely made of painted papier-mâché; dark red suit trimmed with a fur collar around the neck, sleeves and hem; long white beard; yellow sack in his hand and another on his back; 1977.

Although gifts are given to Italian children by the Christ Child, some children get their gifts from Babbo Natale on January 6, the Feast of the Epiphany. Babbo Natale resembles Father Christmas of England.

MARKS: "Made in Italy" on a seal on the bottom of the base.

SEE: *Illustration 249.*

Japan

Japanese Santa Claus: 3in (8cm); painted over enamel and fired; decoration; late 1980s.

The Japanese homes are not usually decorated with Christmas trees at the holiday season; however, stores and public places often have Christmas trees with such ornaments. This ornament was purchased and sent to the owner from her family in Japan. It is now being worn as a coat lapel ornament during the Christmas season.
MARKS: None.
SEE: *Illustration 250. Yoshiko Baker Collection.*

Russia

The area comprising the Commonwealth of Independent States is very large and a variety of nationalities live there. Their legends about the Solstice gift-givers vary widely. Russia is the largest and most dominant of the states of the former Soviet Union, but even it has variations in the stories. Most of the gift-givers in this book come from Russia, but some of their legends extend to the other states.

The names of the Santa Claus type figures include:

1. Grandmother Babushka (see *Illustration 251*). These are usually the traditionally nesting dolls called *Matryoshkas*.

2. Kolyada, a white-robed girl who arrived in pre-revolutionary Russia by sleigh with carol singers and gifts.

3. Deydushka Moroz (Grandfather Frost) (See *Illustrations 252 and 223*.) He is also called Dedt Moroz.

During the period of Communist rule, Grandfather Frost brought gifts on New Year's Day. Traditionally, he came in a sled like Santa Claus, but recently Grandfather Frost has been pictured having his sled pulled through the sky by a Russian Sputnik.

Many people around the world associate the *Matryoshkas* dolls with Baboushka. This is because the small Matryoshka doll-within-a-doll is dressed as a Russian peasant of the last century. Legend says Baboushka was such a peasant.

In 1984 *Matryoshkas* dolls celebrated their 100th birthday. It is generally believed that these small dolls derived from the wooden eggs that Russian peasants made at Easter for many centuries. About 1884, a set of wooden Japanese dolls came into the hands of Russian art patron Savva Mamontov, and he commissioned a Russian version of the Japanese doll.

The name Matryoshka came from Mataryona, a popular name among peasant women at the time. The original Matryoshkas were sold as children's toys and the demand grew. Zagorsk, a village north of Moscow, became the center of making these dolls. Today they continue to be made there, but they are made in other parts of Russia as well.

The dolls first became world popular when they won the gold medal at a toy exhibition in Paris in 1900. They have been sold to tourists of Russia ever since. More than any other form of folk art, *Mataryoshkas* has come to symbolize Russia.

147

Russia

Grandmother Babushka: 6in (15cm); wooden nesting dolls; four dolls inside this one; 1950s.

These dolls have been made for many years. Tourists and citizens in Russia can still purchase them today. They come in various sizes with many different numbers of dolls on the inside of the "nest." There are several spellings of the name "Babushka."

According to legend, Grandmother Babushka claimed that when the Magi were traveling to Bethlehem to find Jesus, they stopped to ask her for directions. She misdirected them, and she was condemned forever to walk the earth giving presents to children.

MARKS: None.
SEE: *Illustration 251.*

Russia

Dedt Moroz (Grandfather Frost): 10in (25cm); Russian gift-bearer; fur beard and hair; red velvet coat and hat with brown fur trim; wooden Russian sled; 1989.

In Russian folk legend it was told that diamonds and ice are like good and bad children. Dedt Moroz turned a Siberian mother's wicked daughter into a pillar of ice, but rewarded her ill-treated step-daughter with diamonds.

In the Commonwealth of Independent States today, Grandfather Frost distributes gifts to good children on New Year's Day.
MARKS: "Buyers Choice//Chalfont, Pa."
SEE: *Illustration 252. Phyllis S. Bechtold Collection.*

The registered trademarks, the trademarks and copyrights appearing in italics//bold within this chapter belong to Anne-Beate.

Denmark

Jule-Nisse: 4in (10cm); all-wood; painted body; red knit hat; 1977.

This small Christmas elf lived in the attic of Danish farmhouses. At Christmas the children set out a bowl of Christmas rice pudding for him so he would not play many tricks on them. The elf's name was spelled many ways including Julnisse, Julenisse and just Nisse.

MARKS: "Anne-Beate Design//Handmade in Denmark" on a label on the bottom.
SEE: *Illustration 253.*

Denmark

Nisse or Jules Nisse: 10in (25cm); all-foam latex; bendable and poseable; dressed in hand-knitted black and white wool sweater and red felt hat; painted red stockings and black shoes; late 1970s and early 1980s.
MARKS: "Latex" on bottom of shoe.
SEE: *Illustration 254.*

Syria

Syrian Camel: 5½in (14cm); carved wood; 1970s.

In southern Syria, the Christmas celebrations include the gentle camel as a gift-bringer. Legend says that camels traveled over the desert with the Three Wise Men. Children leave bowls of water and bowls of wheat outside their door. In the morning they find gifts.
SEE: *Illustration 255.*

Yugoslavia

Polanznich (doll on left): 16in (41cm); sculpted composition head; cloth body over armature; blue wool flannel coat trimmed with brown fur; loden green pants; corn in pocket; carries switches and a basket of fruit; 1991.

The legend card that comes with doll says, "He lets Christ in at Christmas Time. When he comes into the home, he throws wheat in at everyone and at every corner of the room saying 'Christ is born.' This is to ensure a fruitful growing season for the coming year. The mother of the household throws corn or wheat back at him. A coin is then left for his job in the cook arm [sic] that is in the fireplace. Original ethnic representations researched and made by June & Bob Tressler."

MARKS: A legend card comes with the doll.

SEE: *Illustration 256.*

France and The French-Speaking Provinces of Belgium

Pére Fouettard (doll in middle): 13in (33cm); composition sculpted head; cloth body over armature; dark brown wooly suit, gold belt and white cotton gloves; carries switches; 1991.

A legend card that comes with dolls says, "He carries a bag of switches which he leaves in the shoes of naughty children. He sometimes accompanies Pére Noël, The Christ Kindles, or Sankte Nikolaus. Original ethnic representations researched and made by June & Bob Tressler."

MARKS: A legend card comes with the doll.

SEE: *Illustration 256.*

France

Father Star (doll on right): 16in (41cm); composition sculpted head; cloth body over armature; long loden green coat, long green dress, gold trim, and gold net hat made to represent a star; carries fruit; 1991.

The legend card that comes with doll says, "He was the pagan moon god of the winter solstice. He would accompany Tante Aria, who was the Wind Mother. Together they would ride an ass through the night skies leaving fruits in shoes and stockings of good children. Original ethnic representations researched and made by June & Bob Tressler."

MARKS: A legend card comes with the doll.

SEE: *Illustration 256.*

Illustration	Description	Value
Title Page	Duncan Royal (*Thomas Nast Santa Claus*).	$85-100

19th and Turn-of-the-20th Century Santas

1	White Wadding Santa with Die-cut Scrap Face.	$110-140
2	White Wadding Father Christmas and Switches.	$150-170+
3	Godey's Lady Book Father Christmas. Handmade	One-of-a-Kind
	Vogue *Miss Ginny*.	$125-150
4	Ives Walking Santa.	$2100-2200
5	E.S. Peck cloth Santa Claus.	$350-450+
6	Wadding Santa Claus with Moss Basket.	$1000-1200+
7	Santa on Skis.	$90-125
8	Stevens Mechanical Bank.	$550-1150, depending on condition
9	Small Red Belsnickle (doll on left).	$200-250
	Large Red Belsnickle (doll on right).	$550-600
10	White Belsnickle (doll on left).	$800-900
	White Belsnickle (doll on right).	$550-650
11	Belsnickle with Sparkling Costume.	$800-1100
12	Silver Belsnickle.	$550-650
13	Belsnickle with Red Hat (doll on left).	$800-1000+
	Belsnickle (doll on right).	$700-800
14	Large Belsnickle Candy Container.	$3000-3500
15	Art Fabric Mills Christmas Tree Decorations.	Not enough sample prices
16	Hubley Santa with Brown Reindeer.	$800-1000, depending on condition
17	French Walking Santa.	$700-900+, very few sample prices available
18 & 19	Saint Nicholas.	$750-800
20	All-Bisque Santa.	$250-300
21	St. Nicholas by Gebrüder Heubach.	$1500-2200
22	Hubley Santa in White Sleigh.	$600-700
23	Green Cast Iron Santa.	$125-150
24	Santa Claus on Donkey (doll on left).	$1100-1200
	Santa Claus on Elephant (doll on right).	$1200-1300
25	Early Santa Claus.	$150-200

1911-1930

26	Santa Sitting on Moss-covered Cornucopia.	$500-650

27	Belsnickle Candy Container on Sled.	$300-400
	Up, Up, and Away in a Beautiful Balloon.	$60-65
28	Large German Nodder Santa.	$1000-1500
	Pressed Paper Santa.	$50-60
29	Small Santa with Wood Basket on Back.	$600-800
30A & B	Painted Bisque Santas.	$25-100, the German figures are higher in price than the ones from Japan
31	Chalk Belsnickle.	$200-300
32	Schoenhut Display Santa Claus.	Not enough sample prices
33	Santa in Moss-covered Sleigh.	$2000-2300
34	Santa Driving Moss-covered Car.	$900+
35	Belsnickle Sitting on Log with Bag on Lap.	$500-600
36	Composition Santa Claus.	$500-600+
37	Cast Iron Hubley Santa.	$75-80
38	Group of Candy Container Santas. 10in (25cm).	$200-275
	4¼in (12cm).	$250-350
	15in (38cm).	$650-750
	6½in (17cm).	$250-350
	11½in (29cm).	$200-275
	The small Santa Candy Containers are hard to find.	
39	Père Noël with Lantern.	$1500-2000
40	Two Belsnickles on a Pile of Logs.	$350-450 each
	Santa on Donkey.	$900-1000
41	Large Cloth Santa Claus.	$400-450
	Small Belsnickle Attached to Belt of Cloth Santa.	$300-350
	Small Papier-Mâché Santa.	$100-150
42	Schoenhut Roly Poly.	$1800-2000
43	9in (23cm) Bisque Santa.	$300-375
44	Father Christmas with Porcelain Candles.	$1700-1800
45	Cast Iron Santa on Skis.	$50-60
46	Cast Iron Santa Clauses.	$250-350, in excellent condition $100-225, as-is
47	Flying Santa.	$2000, very few sample prices
48	Post Card of Santa in a Dirigible.	$15-20
49	Cloth Santa with Mask Face.	$265-385
	Armand Marseille Bisque Doll in Original Clothes.	$350-500
50	19in (48cm) Santa Claus Candy Container.	$1100-1300
51	Cloth Santa Claus with Fish Net Sack.	$350-450
52	Santa in Metal Car with Stars and Fish Net Candy Container.	$150-200+
53	Advertisement for Santa Claus Filled with Toys	No sample prices available
54	Papier-Mâché Santa Claus with Electric Lantern.	$1400-1700
55	Strauss Sleigh with Two Reindeer.	$1200-1300+

56	Willitts Designs Music Box.	$80-90
57	French Pink Père Noël.	Doll on left $450-650; doll in middle $800-1000; doll on right $500-600
58 & 59	Père Noël — same doll as in the middle of *Illustration 57*.	$800-1000
60	Santa Claus in Roadster Store Display.	No sample prices available

1931-1950

61	Celluloid Santa Taking Off from North Pole.	$30-50
62	Japanese Sleigh and Santa.	Japan $50-55; Germany; $125-150; United States $60-90
63	Japanese Santa Claus on Log Sled.	$110-145
	Small houses in background.	$5-20
64	Santa Claus House with Santa in Doorway.	Santa $50-75; House $5-12
65	Early Japanese Santas.	$75-125
66	Chenille Santa Claus.	$85-90
67	White Rotund Santa Claus.	$85+
68	Chenille Santa Bell.	$45 each
69	Fish Net Candy Container Santa Claus.	$75-125
70	Celluloid Santas (from left to right).	1. $15-25 2. $85-100 3. $12-20 4. $25-40
71	Composition Santa Claus.	$300-400
72	Irwin Santas (left to right).	1. $25-35 2. $30-40 3. $40-50 4. $30-40
73	Austrian Santa Claus with Metal Walking Stick.	$80-100
74	Japanese Santa Claus with Fur Trim on Costume.	$150-165+
75	German Nodder (doll on right).	$200-250
	Mechanical Santa Ringing Bell (doll on left).	$75-85
76	Santa with Snap Hands.	$55+
77	Rubber Santa Claus	$30-40, in excellent condition
78	Santa Claus Candy Container.	$50-70
79	German Santa with Packages.	$150-200
80	Wobbly Head Santa Bank (doll on left).	$135-150
	Old Fashion Santa Claus (doll on right).	$65-85
81	Grinning Santa with Doll in Back Pack.	$250-350
82	Head Moving Santa.	$70-80
83	Candy Container.	$35-50
84	Glass Electric Santa Claus.	$125-175, in excellent condition

85	Belsnickle-type Lamp.	$150-200
86	Jump Jump.	$15-25
87	Coca Cola Santa Claus.	$100-125
	White version, Black version (not shown in book).	$150-175
	Coca Cola Santa Claus (1984)	$40-55
88	Early Japanese Santa.	$75-100
89	Felt Santa Claus.	$300-350+
90	Group of Japanese Santa Clauses.	$65-75
91	Early Japanese Santa Claus.	$150-200
92	Japanese Santa Claus.	$90-125
93	Gund Musical Santa Claus.	$75-95
94	Clockwork Nodder U.S. Zone Germany.	$550-650+

1951-1970

95	Harold Gale Line Santas.	No sample prices available
96	Santa Claus Waving His Hand.	$20-30
97	Lighted Santas.	Santa on left, $15-25; Santa in middle, $30-35; Santa on right, $15-20
98	Post-World War II Japanese Santa.	$20-30
99	Magge Head Santa Claus and the Pixie Book.	$245-265
100A	Group of Hard Plastic Santa Clauses.	$15-30 each
100B	Howdy Doody Santa	$30-40
101A & B	Roly Poly Santas.	$15-20 each
102	A Winter Scene.	$15-25
103	Early Lead Santa.	$75-125
104	Rubber Santa Claus with Green Gloves.	$35
105	Climbing Santa Candy Container.	$20-25
106	Three Hard Plastic Santas. Large Santa on reindeer.	$25-30
	Santa in sleigh.	$15-20
	Small Santa on reindeer.	$15-20
107	Santa Claus Lamp in Snow.	$20-25
108	Large Mechanical Santa.	$550-650+
109	Spring Push Toy.	$15-18
110	Averill *Kris Kringle*.	$125-150
111	German and Bisque Santa Clauses.	German, $50-75; Japanese, $40-55
112	Hard Plastic Roly Poly Santa.	$12-15
113	Mickey Mouse Lamp.	$25-30
114	Hard Plastic Santa Clauses.	$20-25 each
115	Baby Santa.	$50-75
116	Cycle Santa.	$40-50
117	Plastic Friction Toy Santa.	$50-75
118	Santa in a Metal Sleigh.	$40-50
119	Pop-up Santa in Chimney.	$10-15
120	Plaster Belsnickle-type.	$100-200
121A	Sleeping Santa Claus Cardboard Candy Container.	$50-75
121B	Whitman's Santa and Sleigh Candy Container.	$50-75

122	Early Steiff Santa Claus.	$200-300, depending on the condition of the rubber and clothes
123	Climb the Roof Musician Santa.	$50-75
124	Plush and Vinyl Santas.	$35-50
125	Wadding Santas. 1950s-type	$25-35
126	Spinning Top Santa (Santa on right).	$20-25
	Santa House Bank (left).	$25-35
127	Pine Cone Elves.	$7-10 each
128	Musical Carousel.	$50-75
129	Canadian Santa Claus.	$20-25
130	Pink Santa Claus.	$25-30
131	Santa Claus Bank with Lighted Eyes.	$175-225, in working condition
132	Marx Walking Santa Claus.	$35-45
133	Troll (doll on right).	$65-80
	Santa Mask.	$10-15
134	Santa's Elf.	$20-25
135	Wind-up Santa Copter.	$50-55
	Pressed Cardboard Santa Candy Container.	$50-55

1971-the Present

136	Santa and Mrs. Claus in an Electric Wreath.	$25
137	Santa Snow Scenes (left and right).	$12-15
	Middle Santa Scene.	$20-25
138	Pepsi Cola Santa Claus.	$25-30
139	Wizard Santa.	$20-25
140	Hallmark Santa Claus (in box).	$18-25
141	Carlson *American Santa Claus.*	$10-20.
142	Hallmark Santas (left to right).	$8-10; $10-12; $2-3 (not in boxes)
143	American Greeting Corporation Santa.	$4-5
	Yo Yo Santa.	$4-5
144	Santa's Florabelle Flowers Sleigh.	$3-5
145	Ho Ho Ho Santa Clauses.	Small, $5-10; Large, $7-12
146	Applehead Santa.	$15-20
147	*Snoopy* Santa.	$20-25
148	Norman Rockwell *Santa* by Mary Moline.	$200-250
149	Norman Rockwell *Davy.*	$125-135
150	*Snoopy* Bank.	$20-25
151	Bendable Santa.	$10-15
	Santa Claus Ornament.	$2-3
152	Faith Wick *American Santa Claus.*	$185-200
153	Vogue *Ginny, Mr. & Mrs. Claus.*	$100-125
154	Effanbee *Holly.*	$35-50
	Effanbee *Santa Claus.*	$30-35
	Effanbee *Mrs. Santa Claus.*	$30-35
	Effanbee *Snowman.*	$30-35

155	1979 Norman Rockwell Bisque Santa.	$12-15
156	Nutcracker Santa.	$20-30
157	Reproduction Steiff *Santa*.	$200-225
158	*Mickey Mouse Santa* with Walking Stick.	$35-40
159	Battery Operated Santa in Car.	$20-30
160	Pepsi *Stand-up Santa Claus*.	$90-95
161	Annalee Santa and Toy Train.	$45
	Annalee Santa Holding Brush and Wooden Toy Locomotive.	$45-55
	Annalee Large Santa.	$40-50
162	Cleveland Browns Santa Claus.	$5-10
163	Suncatcher Santa Claus.	$5-10
	Mr. And Mrs. Claus on Park Bench.	$10-12
164	Annalee Santa Mouse.	$45-50
165	Tin Star Santa.	$15-20
	Chinese Santa.	$5-8
166	Santa's Workshop Pull-Toy.	$5-10
167	Disney *Mickey Mouse Santa* and *Minnie Mouse Mrs. Claus*.	$20-25 each
168	Civil War (Patriotic) Santa Claus.	$20-30
169	Christmas Reproduction Bisque Santas.	$20-30 each
170	Pantin-type Pull Toy (left).	$3-4
	Wood Pantin-type St. Nicholas (right).	$8-9
171	Nesting Dolls.	$35-40
172	Santa Fe Express.	$25-30
173	Hallmark Santa Claus *Hot Dogger*.	$5-10
174	Walking Santa Claus Ringing Bell.	$15-20
175	Patriotic Santa.	$15
176	Tiny Balloon Santa.	$15-25

Santa on Paper

177	Santa on a Donkey.	$35-50
178	Cardboard Die-cut Santa.	$30-45
179	Die-cut Santa with Lantern.	$35-50
180	Advertising Santa to Hang on Christmas Tree.	$15-20
	Santa Carrying Doll.	$15-20
181	Advertising Paperdoll Postcard.	$35-45
182	Early Die-cut Paper Dolls.	$200-300
183	Wadding Early Santa.	$200-300
184	Santa and Toy Cut-outs by John Gruelle.	$25-30
185	Cut-out Santa, Christmas Tree, Sleigh, Toys.	$10-15
186	German Walking Santa Claus.	$15-20
187	Advertsing Santa for Bank Christmas Club.	$10-12
188	*Kewpie* Santa Claus.	$100-125
189	Pantin *Jules Nisse* and Helpers.	$100-125
190	Large Foldout Paper Santa Claus.	$35-40+, very few sample prices available
191	Advertisement for New England Mincemeat.	$35-45
192	Hidden Words Novelty.	$15-20

193	Santa and His Sock.	$10-12
194	Santa's Stunt.	$10-15
195	Winter Play with Santa Claus.	$25-35
196	Animated Santa Toy Cut-outs.	$10-12
197	Dolly Dingle's Christmas.	$20-25
198	Die-cut Santas with Movable Legs.	(small) $10-15; (medium) $15-20; (large) $20-30
199	Two-sided Mirror Image Early Santa (right).	$15-20
	Kiddie Cut-out Santa Claus (left).	$12-15
200	Slide-a-Card Santa.	$25-30
201	Card, Calendar, Santa Claus.	$8-10
202	Paper Santa Claus Bank.	$15-20
203	Wrapping Paper Santa and Mrs. Claus.	$2-3 per sheet
204	Season's Greetings from Your Coca Cola Bottler.	$10-15

Contemporary Doll Artist's Santa Clauses

205	One-of-a-Kind Jalopy with Santa.	No sample prices available
206	*Father Christmas* by Peter Wolf.	$4000-5000+
207	Santa Claus by Marilyn McElroy.	$150-200
208	Wax Musical Automoton by Deborah Kubilus.	$150-200
209	Birdhouse Gourd by G. Alexander.	$25-30
210	Santa Dressed in a Quilt by Laura Turner.	$200-255
211	Santa and Mrs. Claus by Bessie Kuehny.	$10-15 each
212	Group of Santa Claus Dolls by Beverly Cope. Large dolls.	$400-495
	Small antique reproductions.	$28-45
213	Carved Wooden Santa Claus by Kerin Houseburg.	$80-100
214	*St. Nicholas* by R. John Wright.	$1200-1400
	Seth by R. John Wright.	$1250-1400
	Shepherdess by R. John Wright.	$1250-1400
215	Nature Santa Claus.	$400
216	Folk Art Replica of Antique Toy by Kay Laughlin.	$40-50
217	*Father Christmas* by Judy Tasch.	$250-300
218	*Father Franklin* by Bit of Christmas.	$150
219	Stone Soup *Black Father Christmas.*	$1000+

Santa Claus and Other Bearers of Gifts from Around the World

220	Italian Manger Scene.	$250-300
221	Italian Nesting Santa Claus.	$75-100
222	Duncan-Royale Santas. (6in [15cm], 12in [31cm])	$80-100, $125-130 each
223	Duncan Royale Santas. (6in [15cm], 12in [31cm])	$80-100, $125-130 each
224	Australian Santa in Bathing Suit.	$15-18
225	Czechoslovakian Marionette.	$100-125

226	Duncan Royal Brochure. (6in [15cm], 12in [31cm])	$80 , $125-130 each
227	(Duncan Royal — Brochure only.)	
228	Chinese Balloon Santa.	Not enough sample prices
229	Czechoslovakia Santa with Baskets.	$250-300
230	Italy *La Befana.*	One-of-a-kind
231	*Sinterklas* (St. Nicholas).	$25-30
232	International Bearers of Gifts.	$6-10 each
233	International Bearers of Gifts.	$6-10 each
234	German *Knecht Ruprecht.*	$80-90
	German *Christkind.*	$55-65
	German *Christmann.*	$90-100
235	Austrian Pull-String Santa Claus.	$8-12
236	Caribbean Islands Straw Santa.	$10-20
237	Taiwan *St.Nicholas.*	$10-15
238	England *Mummers.* Lithuania *Zimiemnik.*	$80-90 each
239	England Peggy Nisbet (left to right) *Santa in America; Kris Kringle; Hote Iosha* (Japan) *St. Nicholas* in Europe.	$75-100 each
240	England Peggy Nisbet *Father Christmas.*	$75-100
241	Switzerland Musical Santa Claus.	$20-30
242	Poland Santa Claus.	$20-25
243	France *Santons.*	$35-50
244	France *Père Noël.*	$275-300
245	Mexico Piñata Santa Claus.	$5-10
246	Mexico Santa with Umbrella (doll on left).	$5-7
	Mexico Scene in Basket.	$15-20
247	Sweden *Goanisse.*	$35-40
	Sweden *Tomtes.*	$5-10
	Sweden *Luciafirandet (St. Lucia).*	$25-35
248	Scandinavia *God Jul.*	$50-75
249	Italy *Babbo Natale.*	$50-60
250	Japanese Santa Claus.	Not enough sample prices
251	Russia *Grandmother Babushka.*	$12-15
252	Russia *Dedt Moroz (Grandfather Frost).*	$120-125
253	Denmark *Jule-Nisse.*	$10-15
254	Nisse or Jules Nisse.	$30-40
255	Syrian Camel.	$10-15
256	Yugoslavia *Polanznich.*	$80-90
	France and Belgium *Père Fouettart.*	$55-65
	France *Father Star.*	$80-90

Index

Adler, Kurt, Inc., 83
Alexander, G., 118
American Greetings Corp., 83
Advertising Santas, 103, 104, 107, 109, 110, 113, 114
Amscan, Inc., 87
Animals, 18, 101
Annalee, 93, 95
Applehead, 84
Art Fabric Mills, 14
Averill, Georgene, 66
Art Wood Product, 52
Australia, 129
Austria, 136, 138
Babushka of Russia, 131, 147, 148
Baby Santa, 68
Balloon Santas, 20, 100
Banks, 10, 50, 74, 76, 86, 107, 115
Befana of Italy, 131
Belgium, 150
Belsnickle, 11, 12, 13, 20, 23, 26, 28, 29, 52, 70
Bisque, 16, 22, 30, 66, 152
Bit of Christmas, Inc., 123
Black Peter, 128, 137
Bradford, Inc., 62
Calendar, 114
Candy Containers, 13, 16, 20, 27, 33, 34, 37, 48, 51, 63, 71
Caribbean Islands, 138
Cars with Santas, 25, 34, 38, 92, 100, 116
Carlson, 82
Cast Iron, 14, 17, 27, 31
Celluloid, 18, 40, 44, 45, 46, 51, 65
Chalk, 23
Chenille, 42, 43
China, 95, 132, 136
Christie Mfg. Co., 81
Christkindt of Bavaria, 127, 137
Christmas Reproductions, Inc., 97
Cleveland Browns Santa™, 94
Cloth Santas, 29, 33, 49, 83, 84
Coca Cola® *Santas*, 53, 115
Columbia Toy Products. 58
Composition Santas, 26, 45, 47, 50, 54, 55

Cope, Beverly, 120
Cut-Outs, Paper, 106, 110, 111, 112, 113
Cycles, 69
Czechoslovakia, 128, 129, 132
Dakin, Inc., 53, 88
Delta Novelty Co., 87
Denmark, 136, 149
Die-Cut Santas, 7, 101-104, 107, 111, 113
Dolly Dingle, 112
Domed Snow Scenes, 80
Duncan Royale, 127, 128, 130, 131
Effanbee Doll Corp., 89
Electric Santas, 30, 35, 51, 52, 59, 79, 92
Electric Candle Santas; 30
Enesco, Inc., 100
England, 139-140
Father Christmas, 7, 8, 97, 140
Felt Santa, 54
Fishnet Santas, 34, 44
Florabelle Flowers, Inc., 83
Flying *Santa Clauses*, 32, 178
France, 142, 143, 150
Friction Toys, 69
Germany, 128, 135, 137
Germany, West — Made in, 51
Ginny, Vogue, 88
Godey's Lady Book, 8
Grandfather Frost of Russia, 147, 148
Greece, 135
Gruelle, John, 106
Grup Vom Krampus, 128, 129
HTC, Inc. Japan, 76
Hallmark, Inc., 81, 82, 99
Hard Plastic, 61, 64, 68, 82
Heubach, Gebrüder, 16
Holiday of Canada, 75
Houseburg, Kerin, 120
Houses of *Santa*, 41
Howdy Doody Santa, 61
Hubley Cast Iron *Santas*, 14, 17, 27
Irwin Co., 45
Italy, 126, 133, 146
Ives Walking Doll, 8
Japan, 140, 147
Jules Nisse of Scandinavia, 108, 146, 149

Kane, Magge Head, 60
Kewpie, 108
Kiddie Products, 62
Knickerbocker Toy Co., 68
Knowles, Edwin M. Co., 88
Kris Kringle, 66, 97, 130, 140
Kubilus, Deborah, 118
Kuehny, Bessie, 119
Lamps, Santa, 64, 67
Lanterns, Santa, 22, 35, 102
Laughlin, Kay, 122
Lead Santas, 63
Lithuania, 139
Magazine Cutouts, 106, 110, 111, 112
Magi, 126, 130
Marx, Inc., 77
McElroy, Marilyn, 117
Mechanical Santas, 47, 51, 58, 63, 65, 66,
   72, 74, 78, 92, 99, 141
Mexico, 143, 144
Mickey Mouse Santas, 67, 91, 96
Moline, Mary, 85, 86
Moss-decorated Santa Figures, 19, 25
Mummers, 199
Musical Santas, 36, 72, 75, 99, 126, 141
Nast, Thomas, 1, 131
Nesting Santas, 98, 126
Nodders, 21, 23, 47, 50
Nutcracker Santa, 90
Occupied Japan Santas, 55
Pantin Santas, 98, 108
Paper Doll Santas, 104, 109, 112, 115
Papier Mâché Santas, 40, 41, 42, 55, 60,
   78
Patriotic Santas, 96, 97, 100
Peck, E.S., 9
Pepsi Cola®, 80, 92
Pére Noël, 28, 37, 38, 143
Piñata Santa (Mexico), 144
Pine Cone Elves and Santa, 8, 74
Plush Santas, 73
Poland, 141
Pressed Paper Santas, 21, 48
Pop-up Santa, 70
Pull Toy Santa, 14, 95
Rempel, C. Mfg., Inc., 48
Rockwell, Norman, 36, 85, 86, 90
Roly, Poly Santas, 29, 62, 67
Rubber Santa, 48
Russia, 128, 147, 148

Rushton Co., 53
St. Lucia (Sweden), 131, 145
St. Nicholas, 15, 16, 97, 127, 131, 134, 140
Santons (France), 142
Scandinavia, 146
Schoenhut, cover, 24, 29
Skiing Santas, 10, 22, 31
Sleeping Santa, 71
Sleighs, 14, 25, 36, 40, 41, 69, 71
Snoopy, 85-86
SNP, 79
Spain, 136
Steiff, 72, 91
Store Display, cover, 21, 38
Strauss Mechanical Toys Co., 36
Suncatcher Santa, 94
Sweden, 145
Sweet Dreams, Ltd., 92
Switzerland, 141
Syria, 149
Taiwan, 138
Tasch, Judy, 123
Tin Santas, 69, 95, 100
Train Santa, 99
Troll Santa, 77
Toy Works, Inc., 134
Turner, Laura, 119
United Features Syndicate, Inc., 85
Vinyl Santas, 73, 74, 75, 76, 94
Vogue Mr. and Mrs. Claus, 88
Wadding Santas, 7, 9, 73, 105
Walking Santas, 15, 46, 77, 99, 107, 113
Wanlass, Stanley, 116
Weibull, Charlotte of Sweden, 145
Whitman, 71
Wick, Faith, 88
Willimantic Thread Co., 104
Wilson, Patricia, 122
Wolf, Peter, 117
Wrapping Paper, 115
Wright, John R., 121
Woolworth Company, 72
Wrapping Paper Dolls, 115
Yugoslavia, 150